The OPTION METHOD
The Myth *of* Unhappiness

The Collected Works of Bruce Di Marsico

on

The Option Method and Attitude

VOLUME
1

Edited and with commentary by Aryeh Nielsen

Foreword by Frank Mosca

Introduction by Deborah Mendel

With contributions by Wendy Dolber

DIALOGUES IN SELF DISCOVERY LLC ◆ MONTCLAIR, NEW JERSEY

The Option Method: The Myth of Unhappiness
The Collected Works of Bruce Di Marsico on The Option Method and Attitude
Volume 1

Materials © 2010 by Deborah Mendel
Foreword © 2010 by Frank Mosca
Commentary © 2010 by Aryeh Nielsen
"The Man Who Found Diamonds" © by Wendy Dolber

Dialogues in Self Discovery LLC
P.O. Box 43161, Montclair, NJ 07043
www.DialoguesInSelfDiscovery.com

Disclaimer
The information provided within is not a substitute for professional medical advice and care. If you have specific needs, please see a professional health care provider.

Design by Williams Writing, Editing & Design
www.williamswriting.com

Volume 1
Paperback, ISBN 978-1-934450-01-7

Volume 2
Paperback, ISBN 978-1-934450-02-4

Volume 3
Paperback, ISBN 978-1-934450-03-1

Printed in the United States of America

THE OPTION METHOD

The Myth *of* Unhappiness

The Collected Works of Bruce Di Marsico on The Option Method and Attitude

An Overview of The Option Method

Happiness

Unhappiness

Listen to your heart,
    for that is where knowledge acts.
Do only what attracts you.
Do what you feel like.
Cor Super Ratio. *The Heart above logic.*

—Bruce Di Marsico

Contents

Foreword by Frank Mosca

THE READER OF THESE WORKS IS GOING TO FIND A ROADMAP TO THE vast and varied workings of Bruce Di Marsico's mind. But despite the sometime appearances of complexity, there will be a road sign pointing always, always in one direction: to your happiness. That is the key to remember as you set out on your journey. I know that this is what has sustained and enriched my own journey, one that began decades ago when I was fortunate to come upon Bruce's ideas and then had the great fortune to meet and learn personally from him. This brief introduction is really simply one person's experience of Bruce, of The Option Method and what that has meant in my life.

First at the core, it has meant everything. It has meant ongoing happiness to the degree that I learned to remember my happiness should I forget it. It has meant the disentangling of what seemed to be impossible knots of contradictions, complexities and conundrums that seemed never to yield to whatever I would bring to bear to try and help myself. The image of Bruce like Alexander cutting the Gordian knot of human misery comes to mind. But it was not an act of hubris, but one of immense insight that allowed him to see through the apparent insurmountability of the problem of human happiness. He could then dissolve what stood in the way and open to view that most profound but simple truth: your happiness is always yours; it is in fact what and who you are. Beliefs are the artificial blockages to that direct and incredible knowledge. Questions are the key to removing them.

Like Socrates, from whom he drew some inspiration, Bruce relished the dialogue and the coming to the key "I don't know" moment. The moment when we stand on the edge of two worlds. The one we could now leave behind. The one we have constructed with the aid of culture in all its forms and configurations. Once the veil of our dedication to the pseudo certainty of what we think we know is rent, we are naked to the possibility of taking that giant step to acknowledging the unshakeable truth of our own happiness now and in every moment we are privileged to allow ourselves to know it.

As you read these volumes it will at times seem that Bruce may be going off in endless tangents of discussions. But these are not tangents at all. Remember, that one blinding truth about happiness is resisted by us in almost endless ways. His students and clients raised doubts and difficulties at every turn as they wrestled with the import of surrendering their beliefs in some apparently necessary miseries, some absolutely irreducible requirements to be unhappy. Remember, our whole world rests upon these assumptions. It is no wonder then that Bruce brought his particular eloquence to elaborate and draw out incredible subtleties of argument, wit, pure intellectual power to counter these objections and to continue thereby to hold out hope to those who continued to bury themselves in needless labyrinths of their own making. But he was patient; it was his signature strength. He knew what seemed to us to be at stake, and he wanted for all who would to hear that joy that he himself was living.

So, don't hold back in your engagement with Bruce; he will not disappoint you. In all these decades, he has been my constant companion in life and even in death. His words, his vision, his immense verve in being willing to take on your fears and doubts with extraordinary intellectual skill will get you to that place you yearn for. So it has been with me, through so many unexpected turns and twists my life has taken.

Now in my seventies, I am filled with joy at the prospect of his work being made widely available. He has shone a bright, inextinguishable light into the shadows and darkness of the human condition. Do not fear it. It will not consume but will enlighten and elevate. I am so glad you are taking this opportunity to discover this for yourself. Written with deep gratitude,

Frank Mosca
May 5th, 2010
Hampton Bays, New York

Guide to the Collected Works

The Collected Works of Bruce Di Marsico SPAN THREE VOLUMES, which together constitute his explanation of the truth about happiness: that we are already perfectly happy, and unhappiness is merely the belief that we could somehow not be.

These writings are created from lectures and writings created over a period of a quarter century. Bruce taught a number of extended courses on Option, and this book attempts to follow the general order of presentation in his teaching work, and to serve as a course in The Option Method and Attitude for those who were not able to experience Bruce firsthand.

The course progresses in this manner: first, an introductory overview is presented (*Overview of The Option Method*). This is followed by core Option concepts (*Happiness, Unhappiness, Feelings, Beliefs, Desires, Emotions, Motivation, Wanting, Doing, Knowing*).

Next are the most immediate, everyday implications of these teachings (*Relationships, Believing Yourself, Forms of Unhappiness*), more advanced implications (*Arguments against Happiness, Behavior, Myths*), and then the most esoteric implications of Option (*Happiness without Reason, Enjoying Your Happiness, Option Mysticism*).

Only at this point is *Practicing The Option Method* considered. The Option Attitude is the foundation of The Option Method. Just as "technically correct" music empty of emotion is an empty exercise, so is The Option Method practiced without the Option Attitude. Bruce did not cover the practice of The Option Method until well into his courses, so that the fundamental Option Attitude was well-established in those who used the Method. He demonstrated and taught that once the Option attitude is well-understood, the practice of the Method flows organically.

Finally, *Stories and Meditations* and *A Comprehensive Overview* provide a summing up and review of Option teachings.

The material, while presenting an overall arc of argument, has many loopbacks and repetitions. Bruce often said the same thing in many different ways so that everyone would have a chance to understand the implications of knowing that unhappiness cannot happen to us.

The truth of happiness is simple. Why does it take three volumes to explain? Because the belief in unhappiness takes many forms, and is incredibly complex. But to be happy, there is nothing to know. All the medicine contained within these volumes is to help release unhappy beliefs, and as they fall away, they become of no importance. After studying the *Collected Works*, you will know far less than you did when you started. What you will no longer "know" and believe is that you have to be unhappy. And you will find that, without these beliefs, you will know your own happiness.

The three volumes of
The Collected Works of Bruce Di Marsico

Volume I
An Overview of The Option Method
Happiness
Unhappiness

The first part of Volume I provides an overview of The Option Method, and touches on all aspects of Option, to provide a framework for understanding the details. The remainder of this volume explains happiness and unhappiness: happiness is what you are. Unhappiness is believing that what you are is somehow wrong.

Volume II
Feelings, Beliefs, and Desires
Emotions
Motivation
Wanting, Doing, and Knowing

Relationships
Believing Yourself
Forms of Unhappiness
Arguments against Happiness

Volume II starts by explaining how unhappiness happens. Believing, or predicting the consequences of an event for how you feel, is how emotions happen. Why does unhappiness happen? It is the (unnecessary) use of emotions to motivate your wanting. It also discusses happiness in the context of relationships, how happiness is synonymous with perfect self-trust, and the forms that unhappiness takes. It concludes by dismantling arguments commonly made against happiness.

Volume III
Behavior
Myths
Happiness without Reason
Enjoying Your Happiness
Option Mysticism
Practicing The Option Method
Stories and Meditations
A Comprehensive Overview

Volume III addresses myths: the myths that behavior has anything to do with happiness, and myths such as "the meaning of life." It continues with discussing how we need no reasons to be happy, and then discusses enjoying your happiness, as you get more and more in touch with it (perhaps ultimately manifested as a form of mysticism). It explains how to practice The Option Method to help you or others get more in touch with their happiness. It concludes contemplations on happiness in the form of stories and meditations, and two summaries of Option teachings, one comprehensive and one reductive.

Introduction by Deborah Mendel

The Option Method takes unhappiness from that vague cloud
of confusion and that which just happens to you and brings it
down to the real dynamics that cause your emotions . . . your
beliefs and your judgments.

BRUCE DI MARSICO

FUNDAMENTAL TO BRUCE'S OPTION METHOD IS THE NONJUDGMEN-
tal approach to exploring unhappiness. This attitude, combined with
The Option Method questions, unravels the mystery and "cloud of
confusion" that usually surrounds our emotional upsets. The Option Method helps you let go of those beliefs that are fueling your
unhappiness.

Bruce understood that we are our own best experts. We each have
our own individual, specific reasons for becoming unhappy when
we do. The Option Method questions are designed to help us identify
those reasons. Unlike other modalities, The Option Method does not
require you to rethink, memorize, or adopt a new belief or thought
pattern. The Option Method questions present a painless process
that allows us to simply let go of self-defeating beliefs. The Option
Method reveals the beliefs behind our bad feelings and unhappiness.
Through this process we discover it is painless and easy to let go of
the beliefs that cause our unhappiness.

Did you ever notice that when you anticipate getting upset about
something you begin immediately to feel upset? The moment we begin to fear or predict that we are going to feel any way that we don't
want to feel in the future, we have already begun to feel that way
in the present. It is likewise true of our good feelings. When we are
looking forward to feeling good about something, we immediately
feel good and are in a good mood.

I believe that one of the most profound discoveries that Bruce made in his creation of Option is that our current unhappiness is derived from our predictions and imaginings of ourselves as unhappy in some way in the future—more specifically, our *beliefs* about what we will feel in the future. The answer is not to convince ourselves that our future will always be bright. We know from experience that life does not always work out the way we want it to. The Option Method gives us a tool to question our beliefs and realize that, whatever our future holds, we don't have to feel unhappy about it. When we are free from these "future fears," we will naturally be happier.

Deborah Mendel

Notes to the Reader

1. Whenever an entire passage appears in this sans serif font, it is editorial commentary.

2. Bruce developed Option Method in the early years of his psychotherapeutic practice, initially calling it Existential Analysis, Option Psychotherapy and other similar names. At that time, he was teaching mostly to mental health care professionals. He quickly saw that his teachings—concerned specifically with unhappiness and beliefs about unhappiness—really did not fit into the paradigm of the medical or psychotherapeutic model. They had a much wider application to all those interested in personal growth and development. From 1970 on, he used only the name Option Method. It was his intention to make the Method available to as wide a group as possible so those who were trained could carry on the teachings. Early lectures often included the words "therapist" and "patient," which soon gave way to terms like "practitioner" and "client." These terms should be considered to be used interchangeably.

3. The purpose of editorial commentary in this book is twofold: sometimes to clarify areas that Bruce spoke about during many talks, but did not create any central document or lecture on. Other commentary is meant to provide a roadmap to essays or talks that some have found particularly difficult to understand. By reviewing a roadmap of the teaching first, it is hoped the reader will be able to absorb the works more easily.

4. More resources can be found online. In the archives sections of the ChooseHappiness.net website there are many study guides for topics featured in this book, and audio recordings of Bruce's original lectures. **http://www.choosehappiness.net**

PART I

An Overview of
The Option Method

SECTION I

An Introduction to The Option Method

An Introduction to Option

April 1, 1973

In this talk, Bruce Di Marsico introduces The Option Method.

He illustrates, via a story of a young woman going off to college, that whenever we are unhappy, we believe there is something to be unhappy about. He describes a mother unhappy about the event, a sister happy about the event, and a stranger neither happy nor unhappy about the event, demonstrating that the event does not cause happiness or unhappiness, but rather the judgment of the event does.

He further clarifies that, even in situations where almost everyone would be unhappy about something, everyone has their own reasons. For example, of three married people who are unhappy about their spouses' extramarital intimacies, one might be sadly unhappy that they were not "attractive enough" to "prevent" their spouse from straying, a second may be fearfully unhappy that they may catch a disease, and a third may be angrily unhappy that their spouse violated an implicit agreement.

He then discusses that, while unhappiness is often a successful motivator, happiness can always be a better motivator than unhappiness: love of wealth instead of fear of poverty; desire for changes in society instead of hatred for society as it is.

He also discusses some of the fundamental reasons for unhappiness: unhappiness often arises because of a fear of not being motivated to want what we are already motivated to want. Unhappiness is also used to prove that we're "good" people to ourselves.

We often recognize that other people don't need to be unhappy about what we do, but not that we don't need to be unhappy about what they do.

Not being unhappy about something does not imply being happy about it. Regarding things we don't want, we can be neither happy nor unhappy with them.

ALL of us in one way or another are striving for happiness. We may all have different words for it; we may all describe it as a search for truth or the search for fulfillment, for meaning, for inner peace. But beyond all of that, I guess the word that we use is happiness. So I'm going to sort of use that word happiness as a catchall word. What I mean by happiness is for you to define, that which you are always endlessly searching for, that which you are always endlessly striving for. Some people call it self-actualization; some people call it the fulfillment of human potential; some people call it joy.

Since we all strive for happiness, I guess the big mystery to most of us is, why are we unhappy? And by unhappiness, I mean just what it sounds like: that which is not conducive to happiness, that which somehow prevents happiness; those experiences, those feelings that are negative, that are uncomfortable, that are debilitating, those experiences that are self-defeating. Unhappiness. We have thousands of words to describe it, ranging from mild irritation or a slight disappointment to war and rage, depression, suicide. We have all kinds of words to describe what we feel when we feel unhappy. I guess we're a little deficient in our vocabulary regarding happy feelings. I've been told, by semanticists, that the words for unhappiness far outweigh the words for happiness.

The Option Method is a method of searching for happiness and achieving it. And we begin with a certain kind of exploration of ourselves. We find that unhappiness is not so mysterious; that it refers to some very basic phenomena, which are based on a judgmental approach we have to ourselves and to our life. And if we think about it, whenever we're unhappy about something, somewhere behind that, no matter how quietly, is a voice in us saying: That is indeed something to be unhappy about. Unhappiness, and the experience of unhappiness, proceeds from the belief that there is something to be unhappy about. Now some people believe that there are lots and lots of things to be unhappy about; some people don't believe that.

We've had a tradition in our Western society to label those of us who have been most unhappy with such labels as sick, crazy, psychotic, neurotic—all the psychiatric psychoanalytic jargon—all various ways of describing people's unhappiness. And very frequently we lose sight of that fact, that what we're talking about are unhappy people. And in understanding that, we can understand why that might be so, if we begin with unhappiness, if we begin to look at what troubles us, what disturbs us. As a fundamental concept of unhappiness, we can begin to explore it.

Now like I said, behind all unhappiness, there's a quiet voice— sometimes not so quiet—but nonetheless very frequently a still voice saying: This is something to be unhappy about. And this we call a belief. In The Option Method, we describe this as the beliefs of man. People behave as they believe. Emotions are a kind of behavior. Feelings are behavior; we feel as we believe. We behave as we believe. And in looking at these beliefs, we find that some of them could have been picked up from childhood. And how many of us, as young children, learned that something was bad? Such and such a thing was something to feel bad about. And lo and behold, if that thing happens, what do we do? We feel bad about it. See that it's perfectly consistent for us to feel bad, because behind that bad feeling there's a belief that we ought to feel bad. And so when we feel happy, it's also likewise consistent because what's behind that behavior is the belief that there's something to be happy about.

I'd like to try to make clear how the belief affects the feeling. Let's say you have a situation of a young girl going off to college. She's out in front of her home with her mother, her father, her younger sister, and there's a stranger passing on the sidewalk. And she's say- ing goodbye to them and she's going to college. Her mother is very distraught and very unhappy; there are tears in her eyes; she's feeling very sad. She's going to miss her daughter. She believes that what's happening is really kind of bad; she can't understand why she has to go away to school—there's a perfectly good school in town. Why she has to leave her family, etc. And the mother sees the situation pretty much as something that's to be unhappy about. And so she feels unhappy about it.

Her father, on the other hand, is kind of mixed. He feels that he's going to miss his little girl a little bit and he kind of wishes she was staying home; he was just getting to know her and they were just becoming friends. But he also sees that she's going to be off with her friends at a school that she's very much looking forward to being at, and how it's going to be really helpful to her for her maturity and her intellectual growth. And so in a way, he's kind of glad, too; he's a little sad and he's a little glad that she's going away. And of course the younger sister is overjoyed! She's just imagining having the room all to herself now, and the telephone all to herself, and nothing could be better than her big sister's going off to college. And the stranger walking down the street, he looks at the situation and he feels nothing and just walks by.

Now I use that to show you that there's one event taking place: A young woman going off to college is the event. And yet there are four different emotional reactions to that. There's a feeling good and a happy feeling about it, which the young girl felt; there's a feeling bad or an unhappy feeling, which the mother felt; there's a feeling good and bad, which the father felt; and then there's feeling nothing, which is an emotional state, which the stranger felt. The one event occurred and yet there were four different emotional responses. How do we explain that? If it was the event itself and the event itself was a good event, then everybody should have been happy about it. If the event itself was a bad event, then everybody should have been unhappy about it. If it was neither good nor bad, then everyone should have felt neither good nor bad about it.

We explain it by saying that the event in itself was just an event. The feelings about the event are based on the judgments about the event. And that the feelings we have are a result of the judgments that we make. So that if we believe a thing to be good, we feel good; if we believe it to be bad, we feel bad. Now sometimes we feel that when we feel bad, we have no choice; we just simply must feel bad. That's in the nature of feeling bad. That's exactly what it's all about. Part of feeling bad is believing that we have no choice, that we must feel bad, that we have to feel bad.

There are a number of reasons for this, which we'll explore. What stands in the way of further growth and further happiness? There are lots of things, like lack of self-confidence, despair, and depression, whatever. Almost all these phenomena are a result of some kind of judgments that we're making. And sometimes they're very mistaken judgments; sometimes we assume that we have to feel bad. We just simply assume it. And so since we assume we have to feel bad about a certain situation, we go ahead and do that. Like I said, it's inconceivable that we could do otherwise. Once we believe the thing is something to feel bad about, we are going to feel bad about it. Once we believe the thing is something to feel good about, we will do that. But that isn't a problem for anybody—none of us are suffering from too much happiness. But a lot of us are not as happy as we'd like to be, and we never will be. And that's part of a whole search for happiness—to be happier and happier and happier. No matter how happy we are, we want to be happier.

The Option Method for achieving that is to look very carefully at what we say we're unhappy about—identifying it, whatever it is, however obvious it may seem or however subtle it may seem. Look at it; what am I unhappy about? Is it the weather? Is it the look on that other person's face? Is it the insult, the rejection? Is it the way my boss acted, the way my children acted? Whichever those things are, look at them. What are we unhappy about? And try to identify it.

So in The Option Method, what we try to do is have a person very clearly identify what they're unhappy about. Give it clarity; do not be afraid to identify it. Bring it out, look at it, somehow articulate it. Then after identifying it, we ask the most outrageous question of all, the most ridiculous question you've ever heard: Why are you unhappy about it? And I say it's ridiculous and outrageous because most of us respond: What do you mean, why am I unhappy about it? Wouldn't you be unhappy about it? Wouldn't anybody be unhappy about it? Oh, but that's the secret—that's the point. *Would* everyone be unhappy about it? And even if they were, they might all have their reasons. What's *ours*? Why are we unhappy about it? Just what is behind that?

Without assuming that we have some kind of a fantastic compelling reason, let's look and see why we'd want to do this; why would we want to look at why we're unhappy? Not because we shouldn't be unhappy. No. Because we want to be happier. Because we don't like it; unhappiness doesn't feel good on us. Oh, of course, it bothers other people, and other people would all like us to be happier and we could all go around saying: I want you all to be happier. I mean, now you fix yourselves up and you all become happier, and this is going to be a better world for me to live in. "See, now everybody just go around becoming happier." But that's not where it starts; it starts here, with each of us. If we want a better world to live in, let's at least contribute one happy person to it, one more happy person—ourselves.

And so let's remember when we begin to look at ourselves and we begin to look at why we're unhappy, we're not doing that for anybody else but ourselves to start. If this is going to be a better world, it's going to be better because we're a happier person. So we look at ourselves because we don't like the way it fits. We don't like the way our feelings fit us; they make us uncomfortable.

I had a class this week, and it comes to mind now because I was trying to demonstrate this point. And we used an example about something that most people would be unhappy about. And it was everyone assumed that the person they loved—I think the way it was phrased was: Your wife or husband or lover was "fooling around" with somebody else. In other words, was, according to some concept, being unfaithful or falling in love with another person. And everybody agreed that they would definitely be unhappy about that, if the person they loved was fooling around with somebody else. Okay, fine. So that was a good example; almost everyone agreed that that would indeed be something for them all to be unhappy about.

And the immediate reaction to the outrageous question was: What do you mean, why am I unhappy about that? Wouldn't you be? Isn't everybody? And there was agreement; everyone was. Of course! Why not? So what we did is we had a go-round; I guess there were about 10 of us sitting there. And each person went around and said why that made them unhappy. And the reasons that each person gave were as individual and as personal and as distinct and different from every other person's there, as you can imagine. One person was unhappy about it because it made them feel insecure; it made them feel inadequate. They said they would feel that they weren't really an adequate male if their wife were fooling around with someone else, and that they felt resentment.

Another one said: I'd feel bad because I feel a kind of relief, and that makes me wonder whether I ever really loved her in the first place, and that makes me feel bad. And each person had a different reason for feeling bad—very, very different. One person said he felt bad because he might get a disease. Okay. We can't assume that everyone feels bad for the same reason and that is often a big assumption that we make. And we can't assume it about ourselves. We often do. We assume: Hey, I'm unhappy for the obvious reasons. What are the obvious reasons? The obvious reasons are sometimes not so obvious. And that exploring that can make a fantastic difference, because after we identify the first why, why we're unhappy about this, we get a chance to go further. Okay, well, now why does that make you unhappy? What is there about that? And in exploration, sometimes this is what happens. It comes all the way down to: Hmm, I'm afraid that if I don't get unhappy about this situation, I'll never do anything to change it. And very frequently that becomes the response. "What do you mean? If I wasn't unhappy, I'd be some kind of a rotten person."

An apparently obvious thing, "Why are you unhappy that someone you love died?" brings all kinds of responses from: "Now I don't know what I'm going to do with my life" to "I don't know where my next meal is going to come from," or "If I wasn't unhappy, everyone would say I was no good and that I never loved him, and in fact, maybe I would even think that myself and it would bother me, and if I didn't mourn and I didn't feel terrible, I would be afraid that maybe I never really loved him." And so very frequently, unhappiness is some kind of a proof to us, but "Is it a proof that we need?" we can ask ourselves, since it has such disastrous effects so often, since it's a matter of destroying ourselves, eating ourselves up from the inside, damaging the things that we love around us.

On a grand scale, we know what unhappiness does socially. There's a good chance that if people were happier, there wouldn't be stealing and killing and exploiting and warring. If people were happier, they wouldn't be shooting up on dope. So unhappiness takes a very heavy toll. And maybe it does achieve some ends; maybe it is a motivator. If enough people claim it, it must be true, that because of unhappiness, we achieve quite a bit. Many a man has become a millionaire because he was afraid of poverty. But after he became a millionaire, he never gave up that fear of poverty. And he keeps his million dollars, scared to death of losing it. The fear that we use works against us, even though it works for us. The question we ask in The Option Method is: would it be possible for you, for me, to achieve the same things without using unhappiness to get it? Could that man become a millionaire because he wanted to be, because he really wanted it, not because he was scared to death of being poor? Did he have to be afraid of being poor in order to desire to be rich? How many of us will not go to a doctor because we're afraid? Do we have to be afraid of being sick before we'll want to be healthy?

And there are lots of those examples in our lives, where if we look very closely, we may find that we use unhappiness as a motivation and we become very afraid that if we're not unhappy, we just won't be motivated. The civil rights movement in America is a good example of that. Lots of leaders in the civil rights movement used anger, used a very heightened sense of injustice and outrage; they looked around and they saw injustice. To see injustice is one thing; they got outraged about it. And they did that and it motivated them. It moved them to want to change things. Because they have this fire burning inside of them, this acid eating out their stomach, they wanted things to change; they used that to motivate themselves. The question is, could they have been motivated without the anger, without the outrage? Could they have been better leaders then?

Now this becomes a very real question, because what happened with many of these leaders is they burnt themselves out. Their anger and their fury and their outrage and their great sense of all the injustices got them angrier and angrier, made them more and more reckless, made them more and more alienated from the very people they were trying to help. Some of the most famous civil rights leaders found themselves turning against their followers and saying: You're not motivated enough to change things. I am sick of you; you're just as bad as those who oppress us. Angry at others for not sharing their anger. Turning people away. Before you know it, reducing to a very small radical group. The greatest achievements in civil rights came in the beginning. And since then, not that much has happened. And what has been most productive has been peaceful determination. That is the question: Does anger take the place of determination? Does unhappiness really take the place of determination?

And so if we explore some of the obvious things that we're unhappy about, we just may find that we don't have to be unhappy about them, that we were mistaken. It's pretty much like this: When we were a child, we tasted a certain food and it tasted horrible to us. We thought it was bad; we thought it was bad for us. We thought we would get sick on it, so we affirmed in ourselves and we took on the belief we'll never eat it again because it's bad. Okay, fine. As a child, that worked. It kept you from throwing up.

Now as an adult, is it still true though? Is it still true that we gag on spinach if we ate it? Many of us have been in for pleasant surprises; we found ourselves eating things as adults that we were surprised we could like. We were surprised that they could taste good. Beliefs change; experiences change. Many of us are stuck with beliefs that we've taken when we were one year old, two years old, beliefs that we've inherited from other unhappy people—a whole list of things to be unhappy about. You should be unhappy about this, about that, about the other thing, and we've accepted them and we believe them, never questioning them.

We get lots of support, of course; we just look around us and find everybody else is unhappy about the same thing and we assume they have the same reasons. It just seems so obvious. So we suffer and we take our unhappiness into us and we walk around with it, and it's constantly there and we try to fight it. And once we've agreed that we have to be unhappy about something, there isn't much else to do but to blame. If I'm not going to say and I'm not going to admit that the reason I'm unhappy about something is because of some belief of mine—and I want to be happier, remember; we're all striving to be happier, that's all I really want—and if I'm not going to see that some belief of mine that's causing me to be unhappy, what's the first thing that happens? My finger starts to point. Before I know it, I'm going around like this, saying: "You make me unhappy; you did; this did; that did; the other thing did." And the fingers go flailing outwards and we're blaming everything and everybody for our unhappiness, never looking at the belief that maybe we've outgrown, that maybe doesn't fit anymore, that maybe we don't need.

A well-known therapist said that the whole neurotic struggle was simply one of the neurotic trying to convince everybody else that they're making him neurotic and getting them to change and getting power over them. Convincing everyone of that changes the world. And he said we were faced with two alternatives: Change the world, or ourselves. So many people say: Oh, it's easier to change the world than it is to change me! And we act that way, and we go on a life struggle trying to make our world very small—let's say maybe consisting of a husband, a wife, a couple of kids—making the world as small as possible and getting as much control over it as possible. Maybe a little fiefdom called a business or something and getting control over that. Narrowing the world and then getting the control over it. It seems like the way to become happy, yet it never works because it's the beliefs inside that are going to determine the happiness.

We can spend a lot of energy trying to get somebody else to change so that we can be happy, by using our own unhappiness and telling them they are responsible for our unhappiness, that what they do makes us unhappy. Well, if that's true, you know, then in my story, that little girl that was going off to college, what she did was making her mother unhappy and she was at fault for that. Is that true or not? Well, then she also gets the credit for making her father happy, I suppose, and her sister happy. And of course I'm sure she could take the credit or the blame for making the stranger feel nothing, for being irrelevant to him—that's her fault, too.

So we have a kind of question: does our happiness or unhappiness come from us, our beliefs, or is it actually coming from the events that we say it's coming from? So we look at our own relationships. When we're unhappy with someone we love, our tendency is to point and say: If you'd only change, I'd be happier. Well, of course—no doubt. Because what we're really saying is if you change to suit my beliefs, we'd have no problem, because then my beliefs wouldn't be challenged. But see, I have a belief that when you do a certain thing, I should be unhappy about it. Now isn't it funny that if this were true, that it's the event, how come they don't agree? How come the wife says: "But you don't have to be unhappy about that when I do such and such." How come the husband says: "Yeah, well, you don't have to be unhappy when I do such and such." And we recognize it for the other person.

How many of us will really admit, and agree that that other person really *has* to be unhappy with what we do? Because they love us, do they really have to be unhappy if we're in a bad mood? Do they have to be? Couldn't they understand? Do they have to be unhappy when we're this or when we're that? When we do this or that? Most of us will not grant them that. No, they don't have to be unhappy; they could be understanding. Do we ever ask ourselves this though: do we have to be unhappy? Usually we don't get any further than: "Do we—," and then we say: "Yeah! Of course I do!" But do we? I know we've lived with these beliefs for a long time and so they become kind of obvious, we think. And we think the reasoning behind them is all well thought out, but is it?

And so one of the most fantastic things we can do for ourselves, and it's really a fantastically joyous thing, is to take something that we're unhappy about—it doesn't make any difference what it is. We don't like feeling unhappy, right, so take whatever it is that we're unhappy about—and really go into it. Why am I unhappy about that? What's there about it? What am I getting from being unhappy? Do I really need to be? Why am I unhappy about it? And getting back to some kind of a basic belief, which may boil down to something like: I'm afraid that if I'm not unhappy about it, I'm in worse trouble. That if I'm not unhappy about it, I won't be motivated to do anything. If I'm not unhappy about it, I'm really not a good person.

And so many of us try to prove that we're good people by being unhappy. And unhappy people are unhappy people and they don't contribute much in the way of happiness to others. And we may build things; we may even build a hospital because we're terribly guilty or terribly unhappy. But how come nobody likes us? How come nobody seems really grateful for all these wonderful things that we do for other people? I was such a good person; we suffer so much. How come nobody appreciates our suffering? We've got to drum it into their heads: Look at me! Look at how much I've sacrificed to you. Look how much I've suffered for you. See how good I am! Love me. Love me for making you feel guilty. And we expect love when we give guilt. We place blame and we expect love in return. And it doesn't work and we're amazed. "Hmm, I'm such a good person." And we are good, but the thing is that we make ourselves miserable and no one else notices that we're good. One thing, you know, unhappy people just don't make your face light up. Unhappy people just don't seem to attract other people. So often in our striving to be good we think we have to be unhappy. No. Does that really have to be that way?

So what I'm hoping most to share with you is a question and that's The Option Method; it's a method of questioning. I am definitely not stating that we should not be unhappy. But what I am saying is, don't we all want to be happier? And the question that I'm sharing is, is our unhappiness really necessary?

I'm not suggesting that we have to be happy with disaster. What I was suggesting is asking: Do we have to be as unhappy as we are with it? Do we have to be unhappy at all? There are many things, which we may or may not be happy with, which we may never be happy with, but need we be unhappy with it? And I don't know that we know yet unless we look, unless we ask. Not do I have to be happy, but do I have to be *unhappy*.

Do we need the unhappiness to motivate us to do something about anything? Can we go ahead and do something about it without destroying ourselves as well?

Unhappiness *is* a fantastic motivation. Fire at your backside is a fantastic motivation. But something beautiful in front of you also works very well, and it hurts much less. Because unhappiness does sometime work very well, the next time we want something done, we'll use it again and again and again. And unfortunately, we have a history of that. Wars must work; they must work for some people or nobody would bother. But could being attracted to a more desired state of the world be better than hating the current state of the world?

The Wisdom of Happiness

Do not deny your specialness. You have within you the seeds for a beautiful garden. Spread them fearlessly. Your seeds are not able to grow into ugly plants but only sweet fruits. Some seeds will not seem to grow, others will seem to need extra care, and others will disappear to grow where you may never see the fruit. But wherever they take root, and for however short they seem to grow, know that there was the chance for something that there never was a chance for before that.

Love your wanting, praise your desires, be proud of your feelings, and glad for your actions.
What moves your hand?
Happiness.
What sparks your thoughts?
Happiness in you.
What pulses in your heart with desire?
Happiness.
What gives those desires names?
Happiness.
And Happiness is God.

Your very being is the cause of your happiness—your right to be yourself is happiness. It is your nature to be good. It is evident that you have the right to be happy, always. You are made that way and have no choice. Since your very self desires happiness above all, and since nothing has the power to deprive you of happiness, you have the ability, because of your right, because you are allowed to be happy.

You have no choice but to be yourself. Your self can not be other than good for you, nor can your self act other than in your best interests. Your best interests are anything you want them to be.

SINCE to be truly glad we must believe we are, we have to see this quality as one of our own, as coming from our real self. We have to know that we wouldn't be wanting to be glad unless it was about to emerge from us.

WHEN we are in a situation where we suddenly realize or question our feelings and want to make them deeper or different, let us not be misled into believing that they reflect where we are *now*.
Where we are now and are going to be is up to us *now*.
Where we are now is up for grabs.
Where we are now and are going to be is up to us *now*.
Again and again. Our feelings never reflect where we are right now at the moment we are questioning them. . . . They only reflect where we were *before*.
"Am I glad?"
Pause, heartbeat, smile,
now
"Yes. I'm so glad!"

TRUE Happiness is not the happiness that is sought but the Happiness that already exists.
The happiness that is sought is the permanent avoidance of unhappiness, which does not exist.
Happiness exists for its own sake
and is the cause of all joy and gladness
and is the cause of all wanting to have
and is the cause of all getting.
Happiness is the cause and guide of life and living.

Happiness is not the result of having good things in themselves. What we always meant by *good* merely granted us the right to be happy. Happiness is the right to be happy and is the result of not doubting you have that right . . . no matter what.

All people want is to be happy. Happiness is the ultimate desire. Happiness is the prime mover. Happiness is the goal of all desires.

The desire for happiness is the sole motivation of all people.

All people are allowed to be happy at all times, forever. This is happiness; to know you are always allowed to be happy no matter who you are, what you do and no matter what happens to you.

All people have the right to be happy. It is never wrong to be happy. Those who know it are happy forever.

Blessed are those who know they are happy. Happy are those who know they are blessed.

To be blessed is to have the right to be happy.

To be born is to be allowed to be happy.

To know you are allowed to be happy is to be blessed.

It is evident. God permits you to be happy no matter what or when. Nature permits you to be happy no matter what or when. The only permission you need is yours to be happy all the time.

You don't ever have to deny your happiness ever. It is not wrong to be happy always.

To love is to be happy and do what you want, whatever you want. Be with, don't be with. Smile, don't smile. Be loving, don't be loving (affectionate). Give or say whatever you want, take or ask for whatever you want. You are loving if you are happy, if you are not afraid.

If it is in your heart, where does it come from? Someone who hates you or loves you?

THE best way to spread The Option Method is to live it. Be conscious of the fact that you are living it. Be happy and at peace with all around you. Change what you want, do as you wish, but in all things be happy.

HAPPINESS is the freedom to be as we are, however we are; richer or poorer, in sickness or in health, gaining or losing, winning or failing, approving or not approving, forever. Happy is what we are and what we'll be if we don't believe we are wrong to be as we are.

A LIFE of contemplation is constantly and habitually remembering that you are always allowed to be happy and are indeed happy. You can allow all things to remind you of this. The contemplative life is the source of great joys and miracles.

The rewards of a contemplative life are greater than can be imagined. The Peace that does all things greater than love can even foresee and intend is the natural action of a contemplative. The bliss that is contemplation is your very life.

GOD doesn't love as a special act or intention. To be with God is to be loved by him. The same is true of you, my love.

BEING unhappy is trying to be happy.
There is nothing you have to do to get happier.
Want it and let it happen.
Trying to be happy is the same as believing that you won't be naturally what you can only be naturally.
If you believe that what another is feeling is something to feel bad about—you will.

HAPPINESS is knowing that you are perfectly happy and that Perfect Happiness moves you: gives you breath and life, desire and all you have . . .

WHEN we want to feel a certain way, let us look closely. We will find that we have actually begun to feel that way. To decide is really to discover that what we want to feel we are beginning to feel. To decide means "Don't decide for the past—the future is beginning."

DO what you want, be happy. Be happy and do what you want. Let yourself happen today. Watch yourself happen.

Happiness is in you waiting to get out. The only thing that stops it is believing you have to doubt.

Happiness is here, it is really near, happiness is yours.

Change your way of thinking and happiness will move you now.

THE Absolute Truth is Simple:

There is no such thing as unhappiness.

People have believed there was.

You have been one of these people.

There is nothing, absolutely nothing, to cause unhappiness.

Since there is no unhappiness, and never can be, no one has to be afraid of anything.

There is nothing to be afraid of or angry about.

Nothing that happens can bring about unhappiness.

There have been many symptoms of people who have believed in unhappiness. No symptoms of unhappiness exist, but symptoms of belief in it have.

Once you know the truth that all is happiness, you will have reminders.

All that is can be the cause of your awareness of the truth.

If you believe that unhappiness could happen in any of the many ways you can do that, your body, your mind, your heart, your very self will remind you of what you were believing.

You will not like what you are thinking, doing, feeling, etc.

In order to make the reality of happiness real in your life, there is only one thing to do:

Have the perfect awareness that unhappiness does not exist. Have the perfect awareness that you have changed. Have the perfect awareness that you do not believe what you used to believe.

Have the perfect awareness that happiness is the cause and destiny of all you are and do and all that is.

Every feeling is a reminder. All feelings and thoughts are awareness. Each feeling and thought makes you aware of what you believe about your future.

Keep the faith. Believe in happiness.

Believe that happiness permeates all that is real

and that happiness will naturally manifest itself to you in your life.

Give it room

Make room

Remind yourself *always* of the truth:

"You are never going to be unhappy."

NOTHING causes unhappiness. Happiness is the natural state of man. Happiness coming is the cause of the desire for happiness to come.

Want more and more.

All that you are and have is for happiness to come.

All that you want and have is for happiness to change you.

Let it.

Want it.

Be glad when it does!

THERE is no cause of darkness—but there can be light.

If any ask why there is darkness—darkness remains for them.

If any ask for light,

then when light comes and

"remains" or "cures" the darkness,

we can then see what the light came for us to see.

The darkness was for the light to enlighten.

NOTHING causes unhappiness. Happiness is the natural state of man.

You have found and now have all you have ever sought.
God, Perfect Happiness, Your Life.
All that is left is for you to do whatever you want.
Since you will be happy forever,
in every now,
as you do your life,
think, feel, be, want,
do whatever happens as you.
However you might happen to you,
Do it.
You are free.
Even if your body becomes tied,
your happiness will still be flying within you.

Only happiness can love.

What is it that you are always wanting? Your wanting seems to be like nature. First it wants the tide in, then it wants it out. First it wants it raining, then it wants it sunny. But what is unchanging in all of that?

Wanting to be happy has never, never, changed. Even wanting to be alive comes and goes. Rabbits grow and they die and people and trees are born and they die. Life and death. Even among people. But what beyond that has still been unchanging? The wanting to be happy. Obviously the most insistent, persistent imprint of nature on you.

... Everything in you can change, can come and go—your wanting and this and that. But everything you are and everything you do, you do in order to be happy and that has never stopped. Unceasing, constantly moving, more and more happy.

Expect happiness to manifest itself.
Love it!
Encourage it!

Want it!
Be glad when it does and
ask for more when you want to.

W E have to know that the whole question
of wishing we were more glad,
more happy, etc., in a given situation
couldn't even be a question
unless it was prompted by an urge in our heart.

T o wake up each day is a direct act of God's gift of awareness. Only God awakens the sleeper, gives awareness of happiness, and restores the sick.

God is the only cause of memory for those who forget. Awareness when given is kept and sustained by gladness for having it. Gladness allows a person to do what is necessary to sustain awareness of happiness and health.

If we are not glad, we forget, we fall asleep.

I T is not what the truth *is* that matters. It is what it tells us and what we make of it. It is what we learn from it. For some, the truth of what was or is tells them how things must be. For others it tells us what never has to be again. We *choose* how to use the truth. It is whether we want a future or not. Can the truth of what has been or the way things were dictate how it has to be?

I F you blame no one for your sadness,
you will remember to not accept blame for theirs.

If you accuse no one for breaking your laws, you will acquit yourself at their indignance.

If you are not disappointed that another has not a greater beauty or virtue, you can never feel insulted when you are judged inadequate by others.

If you are not amazed at the ignorance of men, you will always be at peace.

If you are not shocked at the destructive practices of men and the violence of nature, you will enjoy your own vision.

The Creation of The Option Method
and the Nature of Unhappiness

November 1, 1992

In the talks "The Option Method Attitude" and "Functional Unhappiness,"
Bruce Di Marsico talks about the foundation of The Option Method: the Option Attitude.

The Option Attitude includes knowing that the client is always right, that
your knowing why the client is unhappy does the client no good, even if you're
right, and that the Option practitioner is not here to make somebody be happy
who doesn't think it's a good idea.

Functional Unhappiness is pretending to be unhappy because it is a social
norm in a given situation, and then starting to forget that you are pretending!

THE Option Method was created by me (for happiness) as a result
of certain decisions I made.

Sometime before 1970 I decided that people were unhappy because
they "wanted" to be. They believed they should be. I knew that they
believed it was good and necessary to be unhappy about whatever
they believed that applied to; in degrees, to some experience of not
getting what they wanted (what they believed they needed or should
be). This was the way people chose unhappiness as a feeling.

Unhappiness, I decided, was a good term or model word for all
kinds of feelings that people describe variously as "bad" or "uncomfortable" feelings. Feelings ranging from mild annoyance to
murderous rage; from disappointment to suicidal depression. Unhappiness includes the forms of fear of unhappiness like worry,
anxiety, phobia and mania. Unhappiness is a term for the feelings
that people have about things that they believe they need to stop
in order to feel good.

The belief that unhappiness is preferable to happiness (happiness being seen as some form of being crazy), or the belief that not

26

being unhappy was contradictory to a personally held value, is the dynamic of all unhappiness.

The belief goes like this:

"If I wasn't unhappy about it (the loss, or possible loss) it would mean that I wanted it to happen."

"If I wasn't sad (or angry, etc.) it would mean I didn't care."

Fear as an emotional experience, as opposed to a decision and desire to avoid something, is anticipation of unhappiness.

Unhappiness is the fear and rejection of happiness now (for the above reasons of fear of perversity and craziness) to avoid the feared, inevitable, greater unhappiness that will come as a result of such "ignoring" the "truth" that one should be unhappy now.

I decided that *all* fear and unhappiness is the fear that unhappiness will happen. I define emotional need as the feeling of the need to avoid unhappiness.

I describe it like this: "No person is afraid of being poor, in itself, but of being an unhappy poor person. No person is afraid of illness, but of being ill *and* unhappy also. Nobody is afraid of a bear, but of being hurt by a bear; but not of being hurt, but of the unhappiness that is believed will occur from the hurt." The examples are countless but follow this paradigm. People are afraid unhappiness will "happen" to them under certain circumstances. If you were not afraid of being unhappy as a poor person, would you still fear poverty? Could you not instead decide you want to avoid it?

Although all the above may be decided as being worth avoiding, i.e., undesirable, the urge to avoid is not the same as the feeling of fear. The desire to feel well and healthy, for all their benefits, is not the same as the fear of believing that if one is ill and vulnerable unhappiness will necessarily accompany that condition.

I concluded that people create their own, individual personalities in all its aspects and apparent complexities, by means of the beliefs they choose to accept as true about themselves, about other people, about the nature of the world and God, and especially about the belief in evil.

The belief in evil is no more than the fear that people can be made to be unhappy against their will. The belief that unhappiness in any or all of its forms can "happen," or be caused to an unwilling person, is the cause of *all* unhappiness in the person who believes thus.

People call things bad because those things are believed (supposed) to cause unhappiness. They do seem to cause unhappiness precisely because they are *believed* to be bad.

People cannot get unhappy about something they do not believe is bad. Conversely, they cannot *but* be unhappy about something they personally believe is bad.

An equivalent and synonymous belief is that certain things (events, behaviors, etc.) should or should not be. This is also a form of the belief that things can prevent unhappiness or cause it. These kinds of unhappiness range from emotional "discomfort" to moral outrage, tragic sadness or mental "breakdowns" and trauma. Those things that should not be are forbidden, and things that should be are demanded within a particular culture or subculture; not only for whatever other undesirable or desirable effects they may have, but in order to prevent unhappiness which, it is believed, can be caused.

In order to reveal what beliefs are indeed operative in an unhappy person, I created The Option Method. This simple questioning method discloses to the sufferers that they are the determiner of their feelings. It shows that they are feeling exactly what they believe they should feel, always.

It just so happens that when people realize they have a choice in their emotions, it makes a difference to them. People know they don't want to be unhappy when they don't believe it is necessary.

People feel now what they believe they are going to feel in the future. They feel whatever feelings they believe will "happen" to them. They feel now whatever they believe it will be "natural" to feel in the future, even if it is as a result of something happening only now. The current event correlates to current emotions only insofar as it relates to imagined future feelings.

I have created two questions as a simple demonstration of this phenomenon.

"If you believed that at this time tomorrow you were going to be unhappy, what would you feel now?"

"If you were to believe now that at this time tomorrow you were going to become very happy, what would you feel now?"

The Option Method is not unlike the above, but its questions are more specific and personally applicable to the person being helped.

An important point to remember about The Option Method and

me is that I do not believe that people should not be unhappy, or that they should be happy. The Option Method demonstrates that people choose their emotions, not that they should choose differently, but that they nevertheless truly choose, and are not victims to emotions that they have no choice about. Admittedly, these unhappy emotions *seem* to happen to us. That is the unhappy quality of them that precisely makes them so mysterious, and therefore apparently necessary. They are meant to be feelings of helplessness, or we would not consider them unhappy feelings. That is the very belief and fear that they manifest; helplessness, mystery, and need for control over our experiences in order to be happy.

From this, I have defined unhappiness as the feeling (belief) that a degree of happiness is threatened and one is, to a degree, helpless to be happy. The belief (feeling) about the degree of threat, and how helpless one is, produces, exactly, the degree of the profoundness and the nature of the emotion; from slight to extreme.

It is apparent from The Option Method that what people actually need to be happy is the confidence that their happiness cannot be threatened, and therefore they do not need to fear the helpless feeling that happiness will be taken away.

In truth, people's happiness is not threatened in any physical, material or involuntary way. Our happiness is merely believed to be threatened, and phenomenologically, therefore, that is what we call unhappiness; our belief that we can't be happy.

All said, and the above being true, there can be yet another question about the nature of unhappiness. "Can a person be unhappy without, in some way, believing that what he/she actually, naturally feels, thinks or wants is not really what he/she feels, thinks or wants? In other words, can one be afraid or unhappy about anything other than their own feelings?"

The answer is: Absolutely not. Fear and unhappiness, as we have seen above, is the fear that what we will feel (and therefore, now feel) is what we will not like to feel. Feel, in this context, means the emotional experience of feeling bad.

An unhappy person claims that bad feelings happen to him/her precisely because the person believes that he/she would not choose to feel that way, but is instead forced to feel that way by the event—not by his/her own values.

Unhappiness is the experience, read belief, that what I will feel (therefore, am feeling) is not what I would freely choose to feel in this or that situation. The feeling would not seem like unhappiness (would not feel unhappy) if it were acknowledged as what I truly like feeling. Feeling, as we know, means, wanting or not wanting.

Following from this paradigm, we can see that so-called bad feelings come from people believing that their desires are not acceptable to them.

By using The Option Method, properly understood, we will see that people really do accept their own desires or lack of them, but believed that they didn't. It turns out the reason people believe that they don't accept their initial feelings (wanting or not wanting) is because they have learned that they shouldn't, because those feelings are wrong.

All unhappiness is:

1. I am believing that I should want what I don't, and not want what I do. The fact that the opposite of my desires or values seems to be really happening or going to happen is proof that I am wanting or not wanting wrongly.

2. The obvious meaning of this is that I need to be different and have to change myself to be able to be happy, which is to be what I am meant to really be.

It usually shows itself like this:

"My true feeling is that I will not accept or approve of this event. I do not want it, and cannot foresee myself wanting it. Happiness, I believe, is only possible if I change my mind. I am supposed to accept it, approve of it, want it. My position on this will make me unhappy. I am what is contrary to my happiness. I am wrong to feel this. I must not feel the way I feel. I feel sick/ bothered, angry, sad, etc."

Or the protest:

"I believe I am right to want what I want. It is wrong that I didn't get it, or can't have it." That form of unhappiness is showing that the person believes that there are right or wrong desires that should correspond to what will happen. Even though reality seems to demonstrate that he/she is mistaken in that belief, why do they still protest to the rightness of the desire, and the wrongness of what happens? They now feel (fear) that reality is sick, crazy, wrong, etc.

Why isn't such a person happy with that perception, instead of being bothered? To believe that something is wrong with the actual universe makes no sense, even to the self-righteous. The universe is what is, is bigger, and has the final say. Reality is, by any and all definitions, truth. The person feels not so much betrayed by truth, but as missing some understanding he/she needs to be happy.

The so-called understanding that something is wrong or evil in the world solves nothing. It is not an understanding. It just a restatement of the problem. Peaceful, happy understanding would mean that there is no threat to one's own happiness. This unhappy person believes that it is unhappy to not want the universe to be what it is. He/she wants the universe to be different, but believes that it is wrong to want that because the way it is, is the truth. Therefore he/she decides that the world itself is supposed to make itself different, should want itself different, is evil for not being different; rather than accepting the, albeit, puny wish for it to change. "It's not that I (miserable little me) want the world different. It's just supposed to be because that is only right or fair. It just should be. It is just wrong that things are the way they are. Everybody knows that."

By the way, this fear has led to many philosophies and religions to cope by believing that the material universe, or the undesirable aspects of it, is an illusion. Viz. Christian Science, Gnosticism, Shamanism, Witchcraft, Buddhism, etc. This way they are not seen to be against truth. What they are against is, therefore, false and not reality, but only a deception.

The happy answer to this dilemma is that people really do experience the universe, the world, other people, etc. as not giving them what they actually want, *and* (not *but*) they do not approve of that, don't like it, and nonetheless still want what they want. Having the values they have, they can't approve, no matter how much that might seem a harmonious solution. Besides, in that experience *that is the way they want to be.* That is the way they would choose to feel "if" they had a choice (which they do have), and that is the way they really do feel. They are not really at odds with their own values, and the reality of themselves. *Period.*

Also, sometimes people experience the world (or other people) as not giving them what they thought they wanted, and they were glad for that. When they believe there is something wrong with them for doing that, then they are unhappy, of course. What must the truth be? What is the only thing it can be? At the moment they received what they didn't want, or did not receive what they wanted, they changed their mind. We call it "they realized that they didn't want it, after all. They only thought they did." That is one way we describe changing our mind. The truth is, though, that when we wanted it, we did. When we no longer do so, we say that we "thought" we did. This only indicates that what we want, we want, in a sense, conditionally. We are open to better.

The truth that unhappy people believe they should not accept about themselves is the very truth that is intrinsic to a living, wanting being; an otherwise wise and intelligent creature. I am *for* what I am for, and I am *against* what I am against, and it cannot be different. In other words, I like (want) what I like, and don't like (want) what I don't like. I can't be wrong. That is just the way it is. Even if I were now to be for what I used to be against, I would still be now for what I am now for, or the converse. To quote Martin Luther, "God help me. Here I stand. I can do no other."

We are exactly as we wish to be, and would choose to be. We are exactly what we are glad to be. And we can't do anything about that. We wouldn't want to. We don't need to. That is meaningless. We simply won't, can't or don't want to be other than gladly ourselves.

Just because we change our minds it doesn't mean we could or should have changed our minds before we did. That only seems to make sense to those who are already believing that we could have done that: i.e., been against something while we were for it, or the contrary.

For *all* practical, actual, real-life purposes we choose what we feel about everything, and that only feels bad when we believe that the way we feel is not the way we really feel. It is then that we are not glad to feel what we do. The only way we can feel that we are not feeling the way that we honestly, gladly feel is by believing that that is possible. When we believe that we could be at odds with ourselves, be against what we are for, or for what we are against, we will find all kinds of so-called proof for that.

We use our mistakes as proof that we are not on our own sides, we often say that we knew better, or ought to have known better; as if we chose what we really believed would prevent us from having the very thing we were making the choice for in the first place. We always choose to do that which we believe will best get us what we most want. It is self-defining.

To propose that we knew better but refused to bet on what we knew was best is to define wanting as not wanting, and choosing *for* as choosing *against*. That's okay, but believing that is exactly what makes a person "crazy." It is the best description of crazy I ever heard: denying an incontrovertible reality that even the crazy person must know is real. You are who you are. Contrary to rumor, you are not what you know you are not.

This explains the lack of confidence we see in so many people. They complain, "What does it matter what I know? I act as if I don't know what I know. I might as well not know for all the good it does me."

They have made *for* mean *against*, *wanting* mean *not wanting*, *knowing* mean *nothing*, and *real* mean *unreal* or *nothing*. That makes it easy to proceed with superstition and pseudo-mystical explanations of error, disease, life and death.

That kind of unhappiness is believed to exist, but it doesn't, really. People are not against what they believe in. They always want exactly what they want now. People always want what they believe best serves for what they believe is best to want; all values considered. The values that are always considered are those that are believed best to consider, etc. ad infinitum. This is all self-evident when you don't believe that what you feel is not exactly what you feel. When you believe that the opposite is possible, you feel crazy—unhappy. You feel that life is one big problem to be solved. Needless to say, you wait for a messiah or medication or something to straighten out the mess of this world of ours.

In conclusion:

People fear that they are going to feel feelings (have desires for or against) that are alien, opposed to what they would truly want to feel. People believe that they have already felt such unhappiness, and believe that means that they might in the future. All that really ever happened in the past was that they believed that they had felt in a way that they didn't want to feel about not getting what they wanted, but they really didn't. We felt exactly what we wanted to feel, and it didn't have to feel unhappy. We just believed we shouldn't believe we felt how we did. We believed we should not have felt how we did, but we really did. It was what we wanted. Not the unhappiness, but the feelings that would not have felt unhappy if we didn't believe they weren't ours.

People do not feel contradictory feelings or desires. The belief that they do is frightening. People are the living resolution of apparent contradictions. For example: "I love him, but I hate him. What's wrong with me? I hate that I love him."

There need not be any fear of unhappiness here. There is no paradox. You don't like what you don't like about him, and you do like some things that you do like about him. That is the way you want to feel about him. When some of those things you don't like are also the very same things you like, there is still no contradiction. What you don't like you don't like simply for the reasons you don't like it. What you do like about those same things you like only for the reasons you do like them. It is still true that you like what you like for the reasons you like it, and don't for the reason you don't. There is nothing wrong with you, is there, if you tell the whole simplicity of the truth?

It's like cake to a dieter. You like it for the color, flavor, texture, etc. You don't like it for what it does to your hips, or blood sugar level, etc. There is no paradox. You choose what matters most to you and proceed accordingly. There is no unhappiness, no craziness. If you eat the cake it must be because you will accept the consequences. You believe you can afford it. You hope or believe, that in one way or another, you will still get more of what you want. You know you will compensate if it is worth it to you.

People say things like (and feel accordingly): "I don't want to go to work, but I have to." The truth is the opposite. You don't have to go to work, but you want to. The reasons you believe you *have* to are actually the reasons you want to.

"We all do things we don't want to do. It's part of life." The truth is that nobody does anything they don't want to do. All things considered, they'd rather do whatever it is than not do it. Life is only doing what you choose. The rest is what happens.

The only way we do what we don't want to is when we are physically, actually, involuntarily bound and/or forced. If we are threatened, even at gunpoint, we do not have to do anything. We probably will want to in order to save our life, or bide our time.

You are psychologically incapable of choosing or consenting to do something you don't want to do. It is a logical paradox, as well as a physical impossibility.

As long as you don't lie by believing that you were lying to yourself you will see what you really feel and want, and how you always act for what you are for.

There were times, in fact, when you didn't get what you wanted. You know that as far as you know, you didn't get what you wanted. You don't like that: meaning you wanted it to be different. You know that. You will not feel that you want this, this way. You now know that you didn't do all it took to get what you wanted. You didn't know how to, or weren't able to. You lost this one, it seems to you. What about it? What do you want now? What do you want to do now? If you don't know, you don't know. If you want to know what to do about not getting what you want, and want to know how to get what you want, that's who you are, and that's how you want to feel now. Is this unhappiness? How do you feel? Do you feel like the real you? Do you like the way the real you feels about you and reality?

Happiness is being glad for who you are;
liking that you want what you want,
liking that you don't like what you don't like,
liking that you change your mind whenever you think that's best,
liking that you don't change your mind until you really change your mind,
liking that you don't like not knowing how to have what you want,
liking that you don't like being mistaken,
liking that you feel just the way you like to feel about everything you do,
and liking that you feel just the way you like to feel about everything that happens.

Everything is the way it is, and you really can be glad to feel the way you do.

Unhappiness is any form of believing (fear) that when we don't get what we want, or don't avoid what we want to avoid, it means we are going to feel a way we don't want. Unhappiness can also be believing (fearing) that if we do get what we want, or do avoid what we don't want, we will also feel a way we don't want, or a way that's not "right."

Embarrassment and guilt is believing that others will think that we don't mind how we feel when we get what we don't want, or that they will believe we wanted what we didn't want. They will believe we don't care, which we don't if we're happy about how we feel.

Embarrassment or guilt is believing that others will think we don't feel bad, which we don't, or that we feel good, which we do, about something we were seen doing, which they believe they would be embarrassed or guilty about, which they would be, if they were caught doing it. In short, guilt or embarrassment is feeling okay or good, and believing that you can't help it; that it's not the best way to feel. In truth, you wouldn't want to feel differently, but because you believe you could or should want to, you are embarrassed.

This is the root of all guilt, and therefore, of *all* unhappiness: disowning your good feelings. You were who you believed in being, and then denied it to yourself. You felt the way you liked feeling, and denied it to yourself by believing you didn't like it. Because you've done it, and done it many times, you have had to be a mystery to yourself. This is the mystery of unhappiness, of craziness, of evil: the *mysterium iniquitatem* which has plagued mankind from the beginning.

We don't have to believe that things are wrong or bad to be allowed to not like them. We just don't like them sometimes.

The actual techniques and questions which we call The Option Method are discussed in other places. The above is the rationale of the creation of The Option Method and certain insights as a result of using the Method.

The Option Method Attitude

November 11, 1995

I'M good at listening and so one of the things that an Option practitioner is, is good at listening. You can't practice The Option Method if you're not going to listen to the answers. It's impossible because then all you are, is all those other people who have an idea of what should happen; an idea of where this session should turn up and how it should turn out and where this person should go.

All I know is what they say. Now they're saying too much, really. They're trying to tell me something and that is that their unhappiness is infallible, insurmountable and infallible. That it will never fail them. It'll always be there—unhappiness—and that it's invulnerable and it can't be beat.

I guess the same thing is true about Casper the Friendly Ghost. What's your problem then? You see? That's when I have to come back and always help each person to understand, "Well, why are you here? What is it you want?"

See, what you've done is you've put me on the other side. You've made it me versus you. That I want you to be happier than you want to be and I'm somehow wanting you to be happier and you're not wanting to be. That's fine with me. I didn't put a sign up and say, "Hey, Sara Jones, please come in. I bet I can beat your happiness and exorcise your demons." So I go again, "Why are you here and what are you here for?" Boy, is that a relief to them. You see, this person was going to this heady-heady land, thinking that they were dealing with some genius. Albeit I might not deny it, it doesn't apply here.

No, no, I just want to help you with what you wanted help with. That's all. What they saw is that they got help with something and they're afraid that I'm going to start helping them more. That's their fear and that's an honest fear. That's all they're saying: "But I'm afraid you might help me some more with things that I'm not asking for help for." They found they painted themselves into the corner, and that's really okay. I wasn't going to bother them.

So what I say is that, "There is no problem, then? Why are you here now? What would you like from me now?" Here's what I do. If I haven't explained it the moment they walked in the door, I certainly explain it after their first happiness, when they fear that their happiness will be bad for them, and they start going nuts. I say, "What I'm here to do is to help people who want to be less unhappy, to not need help to be less unhappy. That's it. And if you want to keep using me for that so you can be less and less and less unhappy, glad to be of service. But I'm not here to make somebody not be unhappy or to make somebody happy who doesn't think it's a good idea, who thinks it's going to make them phony."

Although I still will ask the question, "Why do you believe that if you're happy, you're in any way going to be against yourself? If when you were unhappy you knew what you wanted, why wouldn't you still know it when you're happy? You knew that you wanted it."

People say, "Well, if I'm happy I'm afraid I won't care." Okay. "Well, maybe that's because you really *don't* care." Oh, you never heard that? Well, that's an essential part of The Option Method. You can't practice The Option Method without having that sense of compassion with a person.

Compassion is the bottom line in The Option Method. That's the absolute requirement and if you ever want to learn to do it for yourself, you've got to be at least as nice to you as you would be to others. You've got to know when you're ready to deal with something and when you're not. And you've got to know when you don't want to question your unhappiness and when you'd be glad to. When you get unhappy enough you'll be glad to.

Like my mother says, "When you're hungry enough you'll eat anything." So even that Option Method which can make you happy, you thought, you haven't used it—you could use it. It's a tool. It's fundamentally a tool.

So what I do in The Option Method is I help people to not need help to be less unhappy. I will help them all the way—there's a few of them over there—to great happiness, tremendous happiness, because they wanted to use the method and they used it and they used it every way.

Nearly all follow-up work in The Option Method is learning its relevance. Where it's relevant and where it's pertinent. It's not to relearn it and relearn it and relearn it and relearn it.

The principle of The Option Method is to take unhappiness from that vague cloud of confusion and that which just happens to you by fate and bad genetics or whatever, and bring it down to the real dynamics that cause emotions, your beliefs and your judgments, and that people who want to get happier and happier don't need to do this all the time.

You see, it's just merely to prove that unhappiness doesn't happen to you, do you see? And that's a powerful step and a big step and that's the step from an old life to a new life—to realize that *you do cause your emotions.*

You can use the word choose, but only in this restricted sense. You cause your emotions by the beliefs you allow yourself to have which you don't even realize are beliefs, which you're going to have to look at to see if they're beliefs or not; to see what you're believing.

SECTION II

How Emotions Happen

Stimulus-Organism-Response

November 1987

THE scientific model we're using is the scientific model of most of the biological sciences. It's called S-O-R, stimulus-organism-response. If you leave out the word "organism," the "O" in S-O-R, that's the scientific model of physics, chemistry, and the other sciences. What it basically amounts to is that for every stimulus, there is a response. There are such laws in physics as "for every action, there is an equal and opposite reaction." The action would be stimulus, the equal and opposite reaction would be response. That's the way chemistry works. You do mix these two chemicals, that's your stimulus; you get your chemical reaction, that's your response.

That's the common model for most of the way the universe works. In science, the mind has nothing to do with it. It doesn't matter what you think about the chemical reaction, it's still going to happen the way it happens. It doesn't matter what you think about the ball bouncing; you drop the ball, it's going to bounce. It's stimulus-response, and the mind has nothing to do with it.

Stimulus-organism-response is often used as a psychological model, and is based on the biological model. For example, you have a plant. It's producing chlorophyll, which is the response, but that was caused by light, which is the stimulus. Actually, it's a little more complicated; it's light plus water plus nutrients in the soil. Light does not *cause* chlorophyll, but when the light strikes or stimulates the organism, what's going on inside the organism now, coupled with that stimulus, yields chlorophyll. So the organism becomes the middle term between stimulus and response.

If the stimulus changes, then, frequently, the response changes. The organism is the intermediary variable. Now, that's a model in the life sciences. For instance, you have the stimulus of food. What the organism does with that food produces the response called growth. Food doesn't cause growth. If I smear food all over you, it doesn't

43

mean you grow. It's got to go into the organism; it's got to affect the organism. And it's the organism that's really doing the responding, not the stimulus, whereas in the other sciences, the stimulus in itself causes the response—for instance, as a transfer of energy. If I laid a ball in the middle of the floor here and I took another ball and rolled it into it, that'd be the stimulus. It would hit that second ball. That ball would move. The stimulus transfers energy, and it's the energy that moves the ball. So the ball is moved by the energy of the first ball that's transferred to it, and its own energy is released and goes on.

The ball doesn't make any decisions. It's just strictly stimulus-response. The idea of stimulus-organism-response is abused and ignored in many of the psychological sciences. For instance, I'm hearing on the news all the time about victims of crimes. "The person is now going to have trauma. The person is scarred for life." These are considered very wise statements by the news, by lay people, but those statements are first being made by so-called scientists, and that's where we're getting them. The psychiatrists, psychologists, social workers are promoting this myth that totally leaves out organism.

There is no scientific reason why someone who has experienced pain, for instance, will be scarred for life. It is just that the rest of society will see to it. But how they will see to it will be through this intermediary variable called the organism. The event of pain on a person cannot in itself cause the response called "scarred for life," or any such thing. It has got to first be affected by the state of the organism, whatever the attitude and the beliefs of the organism are. There is a variable. It is the person. And that will account for why some people will respond differently to violence than other people will, and why people can experience the same stimulus and have totally different responses. We're going to talk about it in terms of beliefs and judgments. But even if you talked about it in terms of their nutrition or you talked about it in terms of their genes, you still have to admit that the intervening variable is the organism. That is what makes the difference. So that every stimulus does not cause the same response in a human being in terms of behavior.

Pain does not have a given emotional response. For each and every person, regardless of what you might want to determine is the reason for that difference, there is a difference. It's that intervening organism variable that we've got to stress here. We've got to think of everything in terms of the organism. Without the organism, the stimulus response is a mechanistic, non-human, non-biological concept. It is strict mechanics.

Now the only response we're concerned with is the response we call emotional behavior, or emotions. There are many, many variables that may lead to human behaviors. But what has got to be clear is that if a human behavior is in any way emotional, the variable in the organism is different than the behavior that is not emotional. For instance, using stimulus-organism-response, in the medical model, the stimulus would be a virus. The organism would be the body's immune system. Response would be symptoms. That's a living organic chain. Stimulus-organism-response. But for those with a deficient immune system, there may be no symptoms. Does a virus cause symptoms? Not even in the medical model does a virus cause symptoms. The virus has to deal with the intervening variable, the organism, and the organism responds. So even in the medical model, a stimulus does not cause a given response, a predetermined response, in cases like viruses. Now, there are mechanical models that sound like medical models, which is if I take a hammer and I slam it against your shin and your shin splinters and breaks, that's a mechanical model. Even though a medical doctor may get involved with treating and trying to heal the broken bones, the actual breaking of the bone is the mechanical model. The intervening variables in there will be the condition of your leg to begin with. If it was a wooden leg, you will visit a carpenter. If you already had a preexisting condition of arthritis, that would affect treatments. If you have hemophilia, that causes other things. So not everybody who gets a broken leg also has the same total biological response.

Again, what makes all the difference is the organism. We've got to keep that term the largest. In "S-O-R," you could imagine a little tiny "S," a little tiny "R," and a huge "O" because the organism is really all you're going to have to deal with. The organism is all we're concerned with. That's all there is for us to deal with. The stimulus, in terms of any practice that we're going to be concerned with here, is not your concern, and neither is the response. You have to deal with the organism.

So I can't underline enough the word "organism." That's the scientific basis upon which The Option Method is based. There are sciences that propose to use this model, S-O-R, and there is nothing in that "O" except their preconceptions and their ideas. In other words, where the "O" is whatever *they* happen to think, and they're not really dealing with the "O." That approach is erroneous, untrue, and not valid.

That brings us to the biological-psychological model. What's true does not matter. It's what the organism *thinks* is true. That falls under this thing called belief. In human behavior, a given event, or more precisely, the perception of the event, is the stimulus. What the organism does with that is what causes the response. So the event, however it's perceived, affects the organism in the sense that the organism has a belief or a judgment about that event. The event plus the belief or judgment yields the emotion or the behavior. This is the model of human behavior: with a given event, the event comes to a person who has a whole system of beliefs.

There are three kinds of possible judgments: good, not good/not bad, and bad. The responses then are happy, okay, and unhappy, meaning this: There's an event, and the perception of it. If the event is judged as good, the response is happiness, and the person is happy. If the event is judged as neither good nor bad, the response is neutral. If the event is judged as bad, then the response is unhappy. And that's the way it works, it's that simple.

You want to know why a person is traumatized, in other words, feels miserable, frightened, scared, unhappy? Well, which one of these three judgments must they have made? They must have made the judgment that what happened is bad. Similarly, all the people who are saying the person will be traumatized; they observed the event, so they must have already judged the event. Their grave mistake is that they believe everybody *must* judge the event the way they do, and everybody *will* judge the way they do. So since the crime victim will judge the way I judge, the crime victim will feel as bad as I feel.

I have summarized this as "Stimulus, Belief, Response." Notice I substituted the word "belief" for organism because that's what we're concerned with. We're not concerned with bloody noses and bad backs and broken legs and stuff like that. We're concerned with an organism insofar as it is a believing organism. Instead of belief, I could also use the word "judgment." The belief that I think something is good is the judgment that something is good, the belief that it's bad is the judgment that something is bad, and not having a belief and not making a judgment is what I call "neither." In sum, human emotions are a response to human beliefs about any event, whether the events be human or not, whether the event is mechanical or physical, even if the event is not real and if it's imagined. Whatever the event is, it doesn't matter, because it is the human judgment, the human belief that causes a human response.

It doesn't really matter whether someone really is a thief or is a murderer or not, but if another person thinks they are, then how they judge thieves or murderers is going to be their response. It doesn't matter then if it's true or not that you're a liar, and if someone perceives you to be, that doesn't matter, either. It's how they judge liars that is going to produce their emotional response.

Don't get hung up on the words "good, bad, and neither" in themselves. These are model words. Does right and wrong exist? Well, for some people that's the way to look at it: things are right and wrong, people are healthy or neurotic.

Nothing really causes any given response except in strict Stimulus-Response. In strict Stimulus-Response, mechanical or physical stimuli will cause a mechanical or physical response. But when there's an organism involved, we're talking about the response *of the organism*. So, if we're talking about a person crying, the person (organism) has the response (crying). With a person laughing, it's the organism laughing. You can't say the joke *caused* the laugh. If the joke caused the laugh, there'd be no such thing as a bad comedian.

Only Beliefs Cause Emotions

November 1987

THE nature of belief in itself is to some degree transient. We've all had the experience of believing things or changing our beliefs about them. If there is a really loud sound, for instance, one person may believe there's a danger involved and will respond accordingly. Another person will not believe there's a danger and respond accordingly. That's not emotion itself. That's not either happy or unhappy or frightened or not frightened. For example, you could go into a science lab, a chemist can make an explosion that scares you, but he's not the slightest bit concerned. He knows it's harmless, just loud. My response to what I believe constructs a whole different scenario about what was happening.

So, the truth of what is happening is not particularly important. It's how I respond to what I think is happening that's going to make me happy or unhappy. What I think is happening is the stimulus to which I am reacting, which may not have anything to do with what's really happening.

Another example: let's say you got upset that a dear friend lied to you, or at least you thought they lied to you, and then they were able to convince you that they didn't lie to you. And you'll say, "Now I no longer believe you lied to me and now I feel better." That is not what an Option therapist is going to deal with. The therapist, and what you want to deal with for yourself, is going to be "But if you *did* believe they lied to you, why is unhappiness the response?" Because the whole world has believed in stimulus-response as all there is, many approaches try to "correct" the perception and thereby change the stimulus. "Lying makes me unhappy. I'm glad to find out you didn't lie. Now I don't have to be unhappy." There is no concept or awareness at all that their judgment is what made them unhappy, not the lie.

Because they've got this rigid judgment that I'm unhappy about lies and happy about not being lied to, the approach is to see if you can convince me that you didn't lie to me, or you didn't steal from me or you didn't mean what you did. If somebody bumps into somebody, then another person may be upset if they thought it was deliberate. But if they find out it was an accident, and the person is very apologetic, "I didn't mean it, I'm so sorry," the response is totally different. But it really was the same stimulus, wasn't it? So really what happened is when you thought the person lied to you, there was a certain stimulus, something they said or didn't say, and you felt bad. Then when they convinced you they didn't lie to you, what really changed? Not the stimulus. They changed your belief about it, and that's really why you responded. They don't see that. They think they changed the stimulus. But they changed your belief about it and that's why your response is different.

It's never been truth or the lack of it that causes emotional responses. You might, indeed, be mistaken about what you think is the event, but given that, what you believe about what you think happened is what causes your emotional response.

People who deal with mental illness very frequently think that the only problem is a mistaken perception, and they try to help the person have proper perception of the event. "No, your mother and father have not been trying to poison you." "Your mother loves you. She doesn't really want to kick you out of the house. She just wants you to behave better." A lot of social workers think that that's their job, and it is also that way in the psychoanalytic profession. Many people in so-called helping professions think that their job is to help change the perception of the event so that the person who would have to feel bad about the original perception, once they have a new perception, they won't have to feel bad about it. "So if you could see that your mother doesn't really hate you, I've done my job, now you'll feel better."

Let me have two volunteers. One, do the stimulating, one do the response. Person one, say something for which person two can have some kind of an opinion or a response to.

Person one: *It's warm out today.*

Person two: *No, I don't agree. It's pretty cold.*

What did you see happening? Did you see Stimulus-Organism-Response? Did person one have to speak? Did person two have to respond? Then you saw the organism. Did person two have to respond? Do you know that person two didn't have to respond? Lots of people don't know that. They never see that part of it. "Of course he responded, he was spoken to." He didn't just respond because he was talked to. I want you to be very conscious of the organism. I want the organism to loom large. The questions were insignificant to what happened. It caused nothing. He did not have to respond at all. That's part of the system of the organism: a decision, a choice. To respond at all takes judgment, takes a belief, which can only be done by the organism. From now on, I'm going to call "organisms" persons, which is what they are in our case.

We're discussing here *how* people get unhappy. Not whether they should, or they shouldn't, or it's good or it's bad, or anything else about it. Strictly scientifically, how people get unhappy begins with a stimulus, which is an event or the perception of an event. It really doesn't matter. We're not concerned with that because that has nothing to do with how people get unhappy. It's either a real event or they perceive an event to be a certain way. It doesn't matter what the event actually is because the unhappiness depends on how they perceive it.

An example: If somebody faints, and I'm aware that they have a tendency to faint, and you are not, I might perceive them as just having fainted. You may perceive them as having dropped dead. That isn't what determines the emotional behavior. I may think that fainting is a horrible, terrible thing and feel very, very bad about their fainting. You may perceive dropping dead as perfectly normal—you're the doctor, and you just think they died and that's that. It doesn't mean anything to you. It's not the event, it's how you then *judge* the event that determines emotional behavior.

So we're not really concerned with the event. I don't get into arguments with a client about the event, or about how they perceived the event. "So-and-so is out to poison me." Who am I to judge? I don't even try to decide whether that's true or not because that isn't the point. And it's not even the point *why* they perceive it that way. You can go on endlessly trying to convince a paranoid that nobody's trying to poison them. That isn't the point. You are only dealing with unhappiness if the event is *judged* as a reason for *unhappiness*.

There's a perception of an event. If you judge it as good, you feel happy. If you judge it as bad, you feel bad or unhappy. If you judge it as neither good nor bad, you feel okay. The event itself is nothing. It doesn't affect the way you feel one way or the other. Those are the dynamics of emotional behavior. It's that simple—that's all there is to it. There is no emotional behavior that does not fit this paradigm. You can have an identical response to two different events as long as the judgments are the same. Some people don't like rainy days, and they get unhappy at rainy days because they're dark. Others get unhappy because they forgot their umbrella. Others get unhappy because it's raining. Others get unhappy because they can't find a cab. They're all unhappy about the rainy day for all different perceptions and all different reasons, but it's all bad. They all judge it as bad.

Now, that's the way emotions really work. This is the paradigm for emotions. That it doesn't have to do with how children are brought up, but with how they judge how they were brought up. It doesn't have to do with wars or peace, but with how people judge wars or peace. It doesn't have to do with nutrition. It is not health that causes emotions; it is what you believe about your health, your judgments about it. Those things are perceptions or perceptions of events. Your physical condition is an event for you that you judge. If you're tired, that's not an emotional state. It's just a physical state. You're tired, that's all. How you feel about being tired? That tired is bad? You shouldn't feel tired? "I must be doing something wrong if I'm tired? I'm not eating right?"

That belief is going to affect your feelings, not the tiredness. Now, the feeling you feel after you've judged your tiredness is bad, you may have even learned in our society to call that feeling tiredness. First you're tired, but now you believe that tired is bad. Now you're going to have a feeling, an emotional feeling in the same body that's feeling the tiredness. So now it's a tired body believing tiredness is bad. You may have learned to start calling that whole feeling tired-ness. You may say, "Oh, I feel tired," but it's tired plus "sick and tired." Sick and tired of being tired is quite a bit different than merely being tired. The judgments can get very much mixed in with the physical sensations, and so then, in our practice, we have to realize that we can be dealing a lot with that.

People often say that, "I'm sick and tired" of this and that, and they actually feel somewhat sick and somewhat tired because they're depressed. "Sick and tired" is an emotional statement, by and large.

All Emotions Come from Judgments
November 1987

ALL emotions come from judgments. If you ignore that judgments of events as good or bad, to whatever degree, are the only cause of emotions, you are unnecessarily relinquishing power over your happiness to events.

Many professionals and the world at large operate on a different basis: that unwanted emotions are caused by events, and therefore, happiness is only possible by *controlling* events. "You don't want to be unhappy? Well, then, stop doing this, and stop acting that way. You don't want to be unhappy anymore? You need to behave as I advise. Is your spouse causing you stress? Be nicer to your spouse. Be firmer with your spouse. Take a second honeymoon. Get divorced." Whatever it is, learn some behavioral way to enforce and control other people's behavior.

For instance, if not having money makes you feel bad, namely, if the stimulus of perceiving that you don't have enough money is the *actual* cause of feeling bad, there's only one solution: you have to make money. If being sick is the only cause of being *unhappy about* being sick, then you *have* to get well. If losing your favorite toy makes you unhappy, then you have to acquire the power to regain it. If the things that we have been told to cause unhappiness are the *actual* causes of unhappiness, then we have to seek power over the world, to control it, so that we only experience the events we desire.

Hence, people in general are very strongly motivated to seek power, not in order to merely have the practical power to effect desired changes, but because power is felt to be necessary in order to have better control over the environment *in order to eliminate unhappiness*. If it really was true that things and events cause unhappiness, then only people with enough power over their environment to ensure it will conform to what they want it to be can be happy. They want things to be the way they seek to have them be, because they believe that *not* having them that way makes them unhappy.

If the only justification for wanting things is "I'm going to be unhappy if I don't have them," even after you get what you want (if indeed you do), are you going to use the same method for the next thing you want? For example, if you made your first million dollars by being scared to death of being poor, will you make your second million dollars by being scared to death of being poor again, or by being scared to death of losing the first million?

Though we've all experienced that getting power doesn't necessarily make you happy, that generally doesn't prove anything to anybody. What people generally believe is that they just haven't done it right. "If making a million dollars didn't work to get me happy, well, I was just mistaken thinking that if I made a million dollars, I'd be happy. It didn't make me happy. I know! I need a more loving spouse. Or maybe a hobby."

But since the emotions come from judgments, not events, every path sought is fundamentally fruitless as a way to *become* happy, even though each path could be a wonderful way for someone to *enjoy* their happiness.

Needing and Wanting

November 1987

THE idea is that you're always needing something in order to be happy. If it is things in themselves that make us unhappy, then it is power that we need. If somebody's insulting you makes you unhappy, then you have to shut them up or avoid them. If someone's assaulting you makes you unhappy, then you have to have power to prevent assault. The idea being that, if it's true that things make us unhappy, we need power then over these things, and so people have often sought power in order to avoid unhappiness. That leads to the concepts of need and want.

These are models. I divide things between need and want just simply to make a useful distinction. Don't get married to these words. We can use the word "needs." I've seen people that I've trained and I've helped scared to death to use the word "need." By doing that, you've distorted what I'm talking about. We speak English. I can say, "I need this" and "I need that." I'm talking about a feeling, the feeling of needing something in order to be happy, that without it, you can't be happy. That's what I mean by "need." It's a feeling, and it's usually expressed one of two ways. I will be unhappy if I don't get this thing. We then say that's the feeling of needing it. "I really am unhappy if I can't get love." That's called the feeling of needing it, and it's a natural kind of feeling that people have. It's a sad feeling, it's a frightening feeling. Unhappiness, basically, is the belief that I will be unhappy if I don't get what I need, if I don't get this thing.

Whether you use the word "need" or not doesn't matter. If you're going to get unhappy if you don't have it, that's called unhappiness. Whereas wanting it, just simply, purely wanting it, I would be happy if I get it. Instead of "I will be unhappy if I don't get it and unhappy if I don't avoid it," it would be "I will be happy if I get it/I will be happy if I avoid it, or I will not be unhappy if I don't get it/I will not be unhappy if I can't avoid it." There are two kinds of motivation or desire: the belief that they'll be happy if they can get it, or they'll be happy if it's something they don't like and they can avoid it. Or unhappiness, which says "I'll be unhappy if I don't get it or I'll be unhappy if I don't avoid it." The unhappy person feels, "I'll be unhappy if I don't get it. I'll be disappointed if I don't get it. I'll feel bad if I don't get it." A happy person is more in touch with, "That'd be nice to get. I'd be happy if I got it." Now, that's a desirable thing.

If it's an undesirable thing like a disease or an accident or a loss of some sort, the happy person says or believes or feels—these are just words to describe feelings—"I'd be happy if I avoided it." An unhappy person would say, "I'd be very unhappy if I can't avoid it. I'd be very unhappy if I don't avoid it." They're opposite feelings. These are the dynamics. Happy motivation is being happy if you get it, happy if you can avoid it if it's something you don't like. So, for the things that you do like, knowing that you'd be happy to get it is happiness. Knowing you'd be happy to avoid it is a happy motivation. Unhappy motivation is using the fear that "I'll be unhappy if I don't get the things I want or I'll be unhappy if I don't avoid the things I don't want." It's a kind of a deal you make with yourself, but I'll call it a belief. So needing is deciding that it's bad if you don't get what you want and it's bad if you don't avoid what you want to avoid. People don't need things in order to be happy unless they believe they do. So if you believe you need it in order to be happy, that's what we'll call need.

The word "need" in English is a very simple word. It always takes an indirect object. You need something *for* something. It always takes the word "for" or the phrase "in order to" after it. You need a knife *for* cutting. You need a sun for sunlight. You need heat for warmth. You need food for life. You need air for breathing. You need money for buying. But when a person says, "I need love," what do they need love for? That's saying you need it for happiness. Well, you could also need money for happiness. You could need power for happiness. You can make anything that you would *want*, *needed* for happiness. So you have very wise people saying, "People need love, people need companionship, people need self-respect, people need pride, people need decent housing, people need direction, people need guidance, people need . . ." Now, these arrogant, authoritarian statements have no respect for the English language or the mind. Need for what?

That's left out. "You know what you need? You need a good, swift kick in the pants." What is the need for? So now it means it's this prescription for what ails you. It's a judgment that there's a disease or an ill or a lack which needs a solution. And sometimes that's used correctly and sometimes it's not. If you're cold, you need warmth not to be cold. But do you need warmth in order to be happy? Only if you say being cold makes you unhappy. Does cold make anybody unhappy? Going back to our paradigm, how did they get unhappy about it? I have friends from Mexico who think it's the greatest thrill to come up to New England to see the leaves change and the snow fall.

The Nature of Choice

November 1987

PEOPLE become unhappy by choice, belief, or judgment. They make a choice of what they're going to believe. If they choose to believe it is good, they will feel good. If they choose to believe it is bad, they feel bad. Why am I using the word "choice"? It's the only thing in life that you can absolutely be sure is not happening to you.

I call this Option method, or Option psychology, or Option theology, philosophy, anything you want to call it. What I mean by it is this: The word "option" is a Greek word meaning choice, decision. To make a choice among choices. The only choices that I'm concerned with here and the only choices that have anything to do with human emotions are the choice to believe that something is good or the choice to believe that it's bad. That's your option. By making that choice, your emotional responses are determined. You cannot choose to believe that something is good and then feel bad about it, can you? You cannot choose to believe that something is bad and then feel good about it, can you? The emotional response is always consistent with the choice. You can use this to see that all these things that seem like mysteries to you when you get unhappy yourself are no mystery. You have never gotten unhappy about something unless you believed it was bad. And you've never been happy about something unless you believed it was good.

I'm going to show you that the experience of unhappiness is already after the fact. When you're experiencing unhappiness, that's the experience of choosing to believe that something is bad. Remember the word "bad" is just a word. It basically means it brings unhappiness. If you look throughout history or anything else, a thing that's called bad or evil—if the word "for" is not after it, as in "bad for," if it's just "bad,"—"it brings unhappiness" is all that it means. Cancer is bad for health of the surrounding tissues. Sometimes it's bad for the health of the surrounding total organism. Sometimes it's bad for the health of the person. But that's all that cancer is bad for. To say cancer is bad is to assume that it is in itself bad, must be cured, must be done away with, and it causes unhappiness.

"Poverty is bad." I have known many, many poor people who are not unhappy. And they were not only not unhappy because they were poor, they were not unhappy in spite of the fact they were poor. They happened to be poor and they happened to be happy about whatever they were happy about. They were happy about their stick houses. I've known people who have no houses and were happy about it, not in spite of it. I have known people who've taken vows of poverty and not only tolerate poverty but seek it out and want it, and they're happy about it. The general belief that poverty is bad, meaning that it brings unhappiness, can be disproved very easily.

I have known people who do not believe death is bad. In our society, if somebody is suffering for a long time with a sickness or a disease, sometimes people see their death as a blessing, you know, "Thank God, they've died. They're not suffering anymore." If death means people don't exist, then they don't exist, and therefore are not suffering. And if it does mean they do exist, who are you to say they're not still suffering?

But what I did want to point out is that it's a judgment, so some people will judge even death as good. I'm not saying that they're smart to do that or it's logical or anything else. There are people who are also happy when people die because they believe they went to heaven. And they really believe it. They just believe that this person has died, has had a successful life, and is now in heaven.

If someone's death causes unhappiness, for all you know, somebody you love may have just died five minutes ago. How come you're not unhappy? If it's the death that brings about unhappiness, then how come it doesn't happen automatically? Wouldn't you have to know about it and judge it and then get unhappy? See, the organism is left out again, the person is left out, the belief is left out.

I want it to become second nature to you that you will never in your life see unhappiness without knowing that what you're seeing is a belief in action. Not something inevitable, not something determined by nature, but a choice. No one is unhappy unwillingly. Lots of things happen to us unwillingly, but our emotions are not one of them. We are not dealing with victims ever when we're talking about emotions. Any client you have who is unhappy is not a victim. Their unhappiness is not proof that they're victims. Oh, they may have been beaten and may be victims, physical victims, but if they're unhappy about the beating, that's their real suffering. That's a worse suffering. And that ultimately is a choice, and the bottom line is, it has to be a choice. That's how people get unhappy.

Some say that the choice was made a long time ago. Perhaps. And aren't you in fact still re-creating and keeping that choice alive? You're still sort of affirming it. I think you're not going to change your mind until you have reason to, and I guess that's the point. We've had many opportunities to question our own suffering in our life and our own unhappiness has been plenty motivation to question; but there's one other thing that's been going along with unhappiness, and that is the belief that it is necessary for our ultimate happiness.

The Most Significant Belief
November 1987

WHAT we're talking about now is how people get unhappy. There is one belief that is more significant than all: that unhappiness is good. And that's why we wouldn't question it, even though everything in you gives you plenty of motivation to question it, you're suffering and you're in pain. Why? The example I use is this: You will take bitter medicine if you believe it's good for you. You'll swallow the most foul-tasting medicine as long as you have the corresponding belief that it really is good for you. You will put up with the most miserable unhappiness because of some belief about it, about the whole nature of unhappiness, and the whole value of unhappiness.

Exploring Some Specific Emotions
November 1987

ONSIDER the emotion of guilt. What is the event and the judgment? It's the judgment that some event, whatever the event is, is bad. What must be the event?

Something has to be called bad before you can have an unhappy feeling. What's being called bad is the event. The original event was: you felt good about something. The judgment is: that that's bad to do. It's bad to feel good about something. That's called guilt. So then we know what the judgment must have been.

For example, consider guilt about stealing. Often when a thief sets out to steal, he feels good about his adventure that's coming up and its possible success. Then when he gets caught and it didn't work out, he feels bad about being caught and feels guilty that he was feeling inspired and felt good in the first place about the whole idea of stealing. So the "how" of guilt is feeling bad about feeling good.

Embarrassment: how is that coming about? What's the judgment? It's got something to do with looking bad now, doesn't it? You're looking around to see if anybody saw that you made yourself look bad. That's the how. I made myself look bad. You can be embarrassed about things that you don't even feel guilty about. If you were all by yourself, you wouldn't care, right? If you were in your own room and you belched, you wouldn't be embarrassed, but if you belched in public, you might be. If you had body odor and you were in your own room and you noticed it, you wouldn't be embarrassed. But you're at a party and then you notice you've got body odor, would you be embarrassed?

It's a belief that you look bad. It may not even be true. I've seen people be embarrassed in front of me, and I didn't care what they did at all. They didn't look bad to me, they looked perfectly normal to me.

How about you're carrying drinks and you trip and fall? We've all lived on this planet, spilling, dropping; it's not unusual or abnormal.

So it isn't really that you're not supposed to do that. In normal situations, you don't necessarily feel you're not supposed to do it. You don't want to, but you don't always feel bad about it. So the perceived event would have to be that I've done something that subjects me to other people judging me as bad or undesirable. But what's the perceived event, the stimulus? It's other people's judgment. You're perceiving that other people may make the judgment that you're unattractive, undesirable. It doesn't even matter if it's true. And your judgment on that is that it is a bad thing. This can lead to now two responses: either embarrassment or anger. If you think that the original judgment was bad, you feel angry. In other words, they had no right to make that original judgment. That could be anger. But if you believe that they're right to see you as undesirable, and they're right to make the judgment, you would be embarrassed. So, if you didn't believe that it was bad for them to make the judgment that you look bad and you didn't believe that that judgment was right, you couldn't be embarrassed. It'd be impossible.

Question: *If I was giving a talk somewhere and I wondered if it's adequate, if I didn't have the belief that the audience might not think I was adequate, that I wouldn't be embarrassed?*

That's true, but what if you *did* believe that they might think you're inadequate? You could think they might think you're inadequate, but if you think they're right or wrong to do that, that is where embarrassment or anger arises. So, for instance, if you're speaking to a bunch of kids who think your story is inadequate, you'd say, "What do they know?" You would not be embarrassed. If you're speaking to a bunch of peers or so-called superiors and telling them your story or giving your report, and you've decided that they are right to say you're inadequate then there is no problem. It's not the judgment that you're inadequate, if you decide that they're right to say you're inadequate. Embarrassment only occurs when you say, "I'm bad for making myself look bad."

The *perceived* event with embarrassment is that you agree that you made yourself look bad. If you agree that you made yourself look bad and then agree that you should not have done that, that it is bad, then you'll be embarrassed. I can agree that in some situations, I've made myself look bad—to a bunch of fools, though. Now, am I embarrassed? No, in fact I'm snotty and haughty and arrogant; I can choose to feel that way, to give you an example. So again, it's still all contingent upon the belief I have. Given the perceived event, that I made myself look bad, that I made myself look inadequate, I have to believe that the way I made myself look, inadequate or otherwise, is a bad way to make yourself look. That I did that to myself and I made myself look bad.

If you saw tripping as a perfectly normal, perfectly human thing to do, and the only real problem with tripping is that you may hurt yourself and that you want to take care of that, what's the issue? If you don't think there's an issue of anybody's judgment there, that nobody has any judgment to make, your enemies will applaud that you've tripped and laugh at you and your friends will try to help you. Where is there room for embarrassment?

But if your friends laugh and you think they're right or your enemies laugh and you think they're right that it is wrong to trip, especially because it makes you look bad, that it's wrong to be human in certain situations and make yourself look bad, then you'll be embarrassed. So it's a form of saying, "I should not have done what makes me look bad. I should always look good." So people can be embarrassed if they dribble some water or they spill a little food on themselves. Whatever is judged to be bad. But more to the point, if you're embarrassed, who chose to feel that way?

Can you see that if you're embarrassed, you've chosen to be? Because most people think that it just comes over them, like somebody has this red blotch they just threw on their face and the heat just built up in their ears. But you chose it. If you're embarrassed, you chose to be.

Physical nervousness is a physical problem. Emotional nervousness is a judgment. If you feel nervous, did you choose to feel that way? Is that the way you want to feel? You must have reasons for feeling that way. Of course you have reasons, but that is the way you want to feel, given those circumstances and given what you think and what you feel and what you believe, that is the way you want to feel. Nobody's doing it to you, so you're left with having to admit you do it. If you had reasons for being nervous, would you then not want to be nervous?

If you're nervous, is that an unhappy response? Is there a belief behind that that can cause that response? You must be believing something is bad. Have you ever been nervous and believing that what's happening is good? That's what you'd call "excited." There's a difference between excited and nervous, and peaceful and depressed, but they're just a difference between judgments. There are two kinds of happiness: peace and joy (excitement). There are two kinds of unhappiness: sadness and anger. In other words, there's an excited state of unhappiness (there's a whole range of names for that) and there's a peaceful state of unhappiness.

So there's active and passive feelings of unhappiness and active and passive feelings of happiness, and they are two sides of the same coin. If you judge the event as good, you're excited. If you judge it as bad, you're nervous. But why *that* agitated state? You choose that one rather than another one. Have you ever been nervous when you weren't judging something as bad? So your question is, "What is the event?" Some event that you would say is bad causes you to feel nervous.

Nervous is the feeling when it may or may not happen. If you're actually sure it is going to happen, there's another kind of feeling, dread. Nervousness—it's an uncertain event. Excitement is like anticipating something good happening.

Bad means, something that's going to make me feel bad. That's what bad means. Something good means something that's going to make me happy; something bad is something that's going to make me unhappy. That's where the decision is. The decision is in which belief. The feeling is part of it. You decide that.

It's all part of the decision of the belief. If you believe that this is something to feel angry about, you'll get angry. If you decide that it's something to be sad about, you'll feel sad. If you decide that it's something to be mildly annoyed at, you'll feel mildly annoyed. In other words, you can't decide that something will make you furious and then just get mildly annoyed. So the response, the actual response you have, corresponds to the belief.

Our Response as the Event
November 1987

S OMETIMES your belief, your own behavior now, or your emotional response becomes a new event that you make a judgment about. For instance, I know somebody that when she feels like she's going to cry, when she starts to feel even the slightest little tears come up in her eyes, she thinks that that's so terrible, and she cries. So then even the feeling that she's going to cry is so horrible to her, so saddening, that she cries over her wanting to cry. But her temptation to cry now becomes a new event that she then judges. As soon as she sees that she's going to cry, now she sees that as an event that she has now made a judgment about. I've seen people cry and be angry that they're crying, really angry that they're crying. I've seen people cry and who laugh at their crying, depending on the judgment they've made on the crying. Or you can bypass the whole thing and just not feel bad at all. Then if you're crying, you know it's not from feeling bad.

Your minds are unstoppable. They're free to judge every single thing that happens, that doesn't happen, that might happen, that could happen, that you can imagine happening. So you know you can judge every single thing or every single nothing. You could judge what might be. So there are people who can work themselves into any kind of a state possible, having no relationship to what's happening. But the dynamics are exactly the same as a person who's responding to what is happening. Sometimes they call them insane: people who have worked themselves into states of great unhappiness over something that has not happened. But how they got unhappy is exactly the same.

Everything can be an event. Our own emotional behavior can then become the new event upon which we judge. So it can go on and on and on and on and go round and round and round. So you can have an emotional response to an outside event and then have an emotional response to your emotional response, then have an emotional response to that. Obsessiveness or compulsiveness is just simply, you will find, a bad reaction to a repeated behavior. In other words, a behavior gets repeated and then the person gets worried or upset that they're repeating this behavior. The more worried and upset they get, the more they do it, because the doing of it was coming from worry and upset either the first time or the second time. There may have been a real, acceptable cause for why they did something the first time. But maybe the second time they thought it was because they were upset. In order to say, "This makes me so upset," they have to keep repeating the behavior. It's like the person who says "shit" and then says, "Oh, I hate saying 'shit,'" and then, "Oh, shit. I said 'shit.'" "Oh, shit. I said 'shit' three times now. That means four times. Oh, shit. I've said it five times."

That's a joke, but it's a version of that. "There it goes again. There it goes again. There it goes again." And each time it happens becomes a new opportunity to make the judgment that it's bad and that it's terrible. It's like, "Don't think of the word 'hippopotamus.'" You're trying not to think of it? Well, that's a model of emotions. If you try not to have a certain emotion, that's the emotion you have. Because, see, there's a belief going on. But the very fact that you're trying not to have that emotion, you have the belief that it's about to come. You don't try to hold back a thief who isn't coming through the window! You only try to hold back that which you think is about to come. So people who try to control their internal or external behavior by holding it back have already enforced it by believing it is coming.

The Cause of Unhappiness
Is in the Future

November 1987

So we make emotions by choice. We'll get into all these which right now you find interesting, all the various kinds of unhappiness, all the various expressions, and there are as many kinds of unhappiness as there are words in the English language. What I basically want you to see is that it is learned. It is a choice and it only happens because of a choice.

I'll start off making what sounds like a cryptic statement. The cause of happiness and unhappiness is in the future. That's all based on this paradigm. The cause of unhappiness is in the future is very simple to demonstrate. If you thought that tomorrow something was going to happen that would make you unhappy, what would you feel now? You'd be unhappy right now about tomorrow. That's a miracle of time.

If tomorrow you knew something was going to happen that you were going to be happy about, you were going to win the lottery, you would be happy now. Why this paradigm works has to do with the nature of believing, and has nothing to do with what *is*. If you believe you're going to be happy, you are happy now. If you believe you're going to be unhappy, you are unhappy. If you believe you're going to be unhappy in ten minutes, you are unhappy. It isn't even these judgments of good and bad; even though that's all true, all that means, though, somehow, is it boils down to you're going to be unhappy or you're going to be happy in the future.

This judgment that a thing is bad is really the same as deciding that something is going to make you unhappy. That's *why* it is called bad. They're the same thing. So now you can take the apparent causality, and reverse it: If you believe that the event is going to make you happy, you judge it as good. If you believe that the event is going to make you unhappy, you judge it as bad. So, *going to be* happy and *going to be* unhappy are really the operative beliefs that are the true cause of happiness and unhappiness right now. You have learned to translate everything that happens into its future implications and then have your emotional response to it now.

The cause of your feelings now is what you believe about the future.

So, if you believe you'll be happy about something that'll happen, it doesn't matter whether it's something that'll actually happen, or doesn't—if you believe you're going to be happy, for whatever reason, you're going to be happy now.

If something bad happened to you today that you were unhappy about, but you believed that tomorrow, in the future, that you will be happy, you automatically start feeling happy.

If you don't judge that anything that's going to happen can make you unhappy, it is not going to make you unhappy. You'll be happy now because you're believing you won't be unhappy in the future and that you will be happy in the future. If you were assured by some miracle that in the future you were always going to be happy, that you'd never be unhappy—and I don't think you have a choice about that—that may seem to go against everything I seem to have been saying, but there is an aspect here—there is no choice. If you choose a happy judgment, then happy responses follow. If you choose unhappy judgment, then unhappy emotions follow. The judgment is the only place you have your choice.

The Choice of Emotions

December 1987

WITH happiness or with beliefs about "should's" and "shouldn'ts," the person is never aware that there is a choice. People say that they don't *believe* they have a choice; that doesn't mean that they really don't.

If your behavior would be considered inappropriate, people will tell you, "Don't do that." Don't act that way, don't feel that way. What are you unhappy about? Why are you angry? You shouldn't be angry at me. They believe that *you* have a choice. You're always right when you're angry and nobody's ever right when they're angry at you. That's believing in choice of emotions.

Up till now, we've been talking about choice in terms of choosing to believe something is good or bad, and those are choices, and that's what determines the feelings. There is no difference between doing that and choosing the feelings directly. People feel the way they want to feel.

The bad feeling is not the physiological feeling, and the physiological feeling isn't making you feel bad. Your response is from judging something as bad, from believing something can cause you to be unhappy. In other words, when you're feeling irritated and angry, you first must have believed you were threatened.

If I believe something is threatening something that I want, I may *do* something about that. But if I believe something is threatening my happiness, I'll *feel* something about that.

For a person to feel irritated and angry, they have to feel that their happiness is being threatened. If you found yourself irritated and angry, you could look at "Why do I believe that thing that is making me irritated and angry could make me unhappy?" You are not free because there's a threat of unhappiness hanging over you.

Look at the most slightly irritated person and the most wildly disturbed person. The threat of unhappiness is hanging over both them. If there are many, many reasons why "if this happens, I'll be unhappy," and great certainty, that's a wildly unhappy person. The less certain the reasoning is, the less frightened the person is, the less unhappy.

"Something is bad" is the same as "can cause unhappiness." "Very, very bad" means "can cause more and more unhappiness." "Slightly bad" means "can cause less unhappiness." "Partly bad" means mildly irritated. "Totally evil" equals being in hell equals insane equals totally unhappy. That's the same as crazy.

SECTION III

An Introduction to Happiness

Feeling However You Choose to Feel

Happiness is feeling however you choose to feel or experience yourself, and not believing that anything makes that wrong.

Happiness is knowing (or not denying) that nothing can make you feel other than how you really do or will feel.

This Is Happiness

1971

This is happiness: to know that everything that is, up till now, is not wrong. It is exactly what has had to be as of now and you did not need it to be otherwise. It has not made you or your life what it should not be, and it will not. It was necessary as a result of what caused it. You are still free to want anything to be (different or not) from now on. It is not wrong that it is and it is not wrong to want it to be different.

When things are not the way you would prefer, that does not mean that shouldn't be happening in your life. It doesn't mean your life is not what it should be. There is no way it should be and you do not need to make it be any way.

Your life is exactly what it is and if you're wanting it different, then that doesn't mean it should not be whatever it is. You're wanting it different means that you want it different. Whatever you wanted or chose up till now is allowed. Whatever you want or choose now is allowed. You are allowed to be what you are. Your life is allowed to be what it is. Your future is allowed to be whatever it shall be.

One Truth

THERE is only one simple truth about unhappiness:

When you believe you are wrong to be happy, you will deny that you are, and feel that you are not.

That is all unhappiness is. Happiness *is* not believing that.

Understand this. Your happiness depends on it. Unhappiness is believing that being happy is being the way you should not be. It is impossible to be happy once you believe that.

People are unhappy when, and only when, they *believe* that being happy would be a contradiction to what they are or want to be or have. When we use The Option Method to question this, unhappiness disappears.

Unhappiness is believing that you are not the way you should be. It is believing you should be unhappy if you are not.

You are allowed to be any way you choose or happen to be. You are allowed to be any way.

Personal Happiness

February 1, 1991

THE only kind of happiness there is, is personal happiness.
Just as the taste in your own mouth is yours alone, so is happiness. There cannot be an objective happiness or a general happiness common to all people. The abstraction can no more exist than, say, health in the abstract. Only each person is able to enjoy his or her own health. It cannot be in another person and be your health.

Happiness, like health, means my happiness. Whereas another's health can be appreciated for the benefits it may afford you, if they choose, the benefit of happiness is personal happiness alone. Even if another were to happily do you a kindness, only in your own happiness could you enjoy it. In other words, your enjoyment is always your personal enjoyment.

There Are No Obstacles to Happiness

September 29, 1990

THERE are no obstacles to perfect happiness.

Nothing prevents happiness. Nothing causes unhappiness. Nothing (outside one's own beliefs) makes a person believe in unhappiness.

All beliefs are choices to accept as true that which is proposed as true; i.e., what "seems" evident.

What seems evident may only seem evident because of previous beliefs of what is true. Assumed facts or false premises can lead to the mistakes that appear to be "evidence," but are merely logical deductions or interpretations based on those false assumptions.

One universal false assumption *is* that our unhappiness happens against our will or desire, and not by our choice. The choice involved here is the choice to believe that false assumption. Once believed, it will seem that unhappiness happens to us.

The belief that not getting what you want (subject to degrees of personal relative importance) makes you unhappy (according to those same degrees of value) is the belief that is the actual cause of the unhappiness. For example, the greater the subjective loss, the greater the sadness. The greater the supposed insult, the greater the anger, etc. Can a person be unhappy about something they do not believe is something to be unhappy about?

The universal belief underlying all the errors and assumptions of unhappiness is this one simple belief: Happiness is wrong at certain times or under certain circumstances and conditions. Therefore, unhappiness is felt.

SECTION IV

An Introduction to Unhappiness

The Cause of Unhappiness

1970

THE cause of unhappiness is a belief. What happens, no matter how undesirable or destructive to our life, health, desires or loves, does not cause unhappiness. The belief that we have to be unhappy is the only cause.

To state it simply: If a person did not believe he or she had to be unhappy, they would not and could not be.

We merely believe we need to have things or avoid things in order to avoid unhappiness, which we would not have to fear if we did not believe we needed to be unhappy.

Unhappiness Is Believing that
You Are against Yourself

UNHAPPINESS is believing that you are against yourself.
Unhappiness is believing that something means you are against yourself.

Unhappiness is believing that something you want or not means you are against yourself.

Unhappiness is believing that something you want or not means you are against yourself and your future happiness.

Unhappiness is believing that something you think or not means you are against yourself and your future happiness.

Unhappiness is believing that something you do or not means you are against yourself and your future happiness.

Unhappiness is believing that you are not the way you should be.

Unhappiness is believing that being happy is being not the way you should be.

What Causes Unhappiness?

The Seven Understandings of All Unhappiness

1. Unhappiness is the feeling of a belief about a perceived or imagined phenomenon; not an experience caused by the phenomenon or anything else.
2. Unhappiness is experiencing your own believing that an event is bad and/or should not be because you believe IT causes unhappiness.
3. Believing something causes unhappiness is the very reason it seems to "cause" unhappiness.
4. Believing that something can cause unhappiness is the only cause of the fear of it. By "fear" is meant loathing, need to avoid, need to cure, need to kill or eliminate, disgust, hatred, terror, horror, repulsion, disdain and all such similar feelings. (Fear is not a simple desire to avoid, destroy, or otherwise prevent or eliminate a threat to your desired values. That attitude does not need to presume avoiding unhappiness in order to justify a simple desire.)
5. Believing someone or something is morally wrong or evil, psychologically "sick," or behaviorally inappropriate is to fear that person or thing as if it could cause unhappiness.
6. Unhappiness is fearing that unhappiness can "happen" or be caused by anything.
7. Unhappiness is believing that something is necessary, something has to be, should be, ought to be, or must be other than what it is.

WHEN a person is believing he/she has to be unhappy, what they are believing is that they have to be unhappy because they believe they are against themselves. The belief in unhappiness is the belief in being wrong for oneself. Unhappiness, in fact, means that I believe that I do, or want, or think, or feel a way that is bad for me.

A person believes: certain things I do not want to happen may happen or are now happening. I don't want them to. I feel bad (and am worried or afraid now) because I shouldn't be thinking negatively about my life now. Maybe I shouldn't be not wanting what is evidently happening anyway. I am (as-if) denying reality, and that is wrong. I will be unhappy about this in the future because when certain things I do not want or do not like happen I will feel a way that is bad for me. It is wrong to expect misfortune. That is "unhappy" of me.

It doesn't matter that if the undesirable event happens to me from circumstances out of my control, or if I think I am the cause or part of the cause; unhappiness comes as me believing that I now have proof that I am bad for myself.

"Bad for myself" means I am not really wanting for me what I "should" be wanting for me, and something can prove it. The belief is that this event "proves" it.

Basically, feeling bad means that I believe that what I do, or think, or want, or feel means I am against my own best interests. I believe these are a bad way of doing, thinking, wanting or feeling. The way I am being is a bad (wrong, self-defeating) way of being.

This could be called the same as believing that I will be a way I shouldn't be, or think a way I shouldn't, or want or feel a way I shouldn't. If we didn't believe that we could be a way we "shouldn't," we couldn't feel unhappy no matter what else we felt.

All unhappiness is the fear that we have a bad attitude for ourselves. We are afraid that something proves we are bad for ourselves in the sense that we are in some way against what we are for, and for what we are against. We are afraid that we have a self-defeating attitude.

The fear that we have a bad, or self-defeating, attitude is the same as distrusting the very source or cause of our motivation. We are unhappy when we believe our very life, our heart, our self is against all that we live for; our personal happiness.

Happiness is the freedom to be as we are, however we are; richer or poorer, in sickness or in health, gaining or losing, succeeding or failing, wanting or not wanting, approving or not approving, forever. Happy is what we are and what we'll be if we don't believe we are wrong to be as we are.

Proof We Are "Bad"

ALL unhappiness is caused by the belief in "proof that we shouldn't be happy"; which really means "proof" that we shouldn't have been free to have been as we were, which is why we are as we are. The undesirable incident "proves," "shows" or "makes it be" that we are bad for ourselves. The belief that we could in any way be bad for ourselves is unhappiness. Anyone who believes that is, by definition, unhappy.

People are either sad or angry at this proof. Sadness is the acceptance of such proof. Sadness is believing that what is proved is that they are unable to be other than against themselves. They can't help it.

Anger is believing that they are being made to be against themselves, and it should not have been necessary for it to have happened at this time. They believe that not only are they against themselves, but it was caused by their not admitting or expecting to be disappointed at this time. Anger is feeling wrong for not expecting to be wrong. They feel they fooled themselves. People can seem to be angry at themselves or at another. They are really angry that *they* allowed themselves to be mistaken.

People are angry at being fooled when they "shouldn't" be. In short, anger is believing in being tricked into being self-defeating. The archetypical case is finding oneself being punished for doing what was believed was a "good" deed.

Sadness is feeling bad about losing something or someone we believe we need for our happiness. Without it we believe we have less "proof of our goodness" for ourselves.

Are You Good? Are All Things Good?

IN the moral sense it would have to follow that everything that is, including yourself, is truly good, in that nothing is bad.

If good is better than not bad, and is supposed to be a "proof that you are truly good for yourself, and proof therefore of your right to be happy," then you will need to know that everything is proof of your goodness and holiness; thereby understanding all as causing happiness.

Your very being is the cause of your happiness—your right to be yourself is happiness. It is your nature to be good. It is evident that you have the right to be happy, always. You are made that way and have no choice. Since your very self desires happiness above all, and since nothing has the power to deprive you of happiness, you have the ability, because of your right, because you are allowed to be happy.

You have no choice but to be yourself. Your self cannot be other than good for you, nor can your self act other than in your best interests. Your best interests are anything you want them to be. Your self defines your best interests in the way that you are best satisfied is best. You will always agree with your self as to what your best interest is, and will always be motivated accordingly.

You always agree with yourself, perfectly, and never do not. You have no choice. Don't be ashamed of anything you are. You are in perfect conformity with the cause of your being. In religious terms, you are exactly the way God wants you to be, and you need not, nor cannot be otherwise.

Do anything, or don't do anything, now or at any time. You can never harm or diminish the happiness in your future. You can always expect to be happier and happier.

All people are good and can do no evil, but all believe otherwise. All have the right to be happy. They have no choice.

To live in joy and peace is the happy reality.

Acting Unhappy

THE difference between acting as if you were unhappy, for whatever reason, and being unhappy is that acting does not include believing that it would be bad or wrong to be happy. An actor doesn't believe he is not really happy. He denies his happiness to another but not to himself.

When you are done being unhappy you can just admit that you made yourself "feel" that you were and are not really unhappy. There is no being really unhappy. There was only believing it was wrong to be happy.

Pretending to Be Unhappy

August 1979

ARE there things which can usually be happily achieved that at times others will not allow us to have unless we are truly unhappy? Is there anything that we could want that we would have to be unhappy in order to get? Can we pretend to be angry in order to be believable that we truly want what we want? Can we pretend to be sad in order to be believable that we truly want what we want? Is pretending unhappiness in any case real unhappiness?

It is only unhappiness if you are angry that they seem to require sadness or anger, or are sad that they seem to need greater proof of your sincerity and determination.

So what if another does not believe you will go to such "extremes" to get what you want? They believe they should know the limits of happiness. They believe that happiness must be lost when a person goes "too far" or is "too careful." They believe certain tasks require worry or fear in order to do them. They invent concepts of "uptight, impatient, compulsive" to put down certain desires they consider dangerous to peace of mind.

On the other hand, they also invent concepts of "lazy, phobic, timid" to put down certain lacks of desire they consider dangerous to happiness: too ambitious or too lazy, too driven or too apathetic, too manic (uptight, anxious) or depressed (lazy, uncaring).

Functional Unhappiness

November 11, 1995

ONE could have the very happy experience for instance of thinking that they might be unhappy, looking at what they're believing, and finding that they don't have such a belief to produce such a feeling, and therefore what? They're not unhappy and that is a great relief.

What they are is functionally, illusionally unhappy because they're afraid they're unhappy and that fear works as well as any other as a fear, but it doesn't mean that it has any basis in their own experience.

So in other words if you mistake your own experience and then you realize that you've mistaken your own experience, any judgments you've made on that are gone. If you mistook somebody for your sister and you went up to kiss them and you saw they weren't your sister, all those feelings usually are gone, replaced by other kinds, if she's pretty or not. But that's it.

When the thing is seen to be as your own illusion, you don't credit it with the same validity. You say, "Oh, that's only my illusion," or "That's my dream" or "That was my belief." So, that's what one can do. One can explore one's feelings, find out there are no beliefs about them, no unhappy beliefs involved, there's no belief that you should be feeling that way, and then ask yourself, "Then what's the problem?"

I've seen a lot of questions here, sometimes, about symptoms of unhappiness. You didn't call them that, but I do. The first thing you learn is that symptoms are something to be unhappy about. If they're symptoms of unhappiness or if they're symptoms of disease, are they still anything to be unhappy about, in and of themselves, and why do you believe they are?

So it could be that people who are afraid of so-called unhappiness symptoms, that feel bad about having symptoms of unhappiness, are just simply that. They feel bad about having symptoms of unhappiness, especially when they don't have any reason to be unhappy, except now they're feeling bad about having symptoms for being unhappy. You see, they think they saw symptoms.

I often meet with people who believe that they're unhappy and aren't. I mean, that may sound funny. Yes, they're unhappy but they really aren't. They come and tell me all these symptoms they had about this and that and they're excited really or they're horny or they're just very peaceful and quiet when everybody else is being all riled up or they're all frenetic when everybody else is all calmed down.

People who worry about their feelings, you see, that's a worry. That's true because they're worried about their feelings, but they're worried that those feelings are unhappy or they're wrong. Many times those feelings aren't unhappy feelings. They're exactly what they are. A person is at peace and calm and everybody else is all hyped up and saying, "What's the matter with you. Why aren't you getting all riled up? Why aren't you happy?"

Questioner: *But now that worry is, now what I'm experiencing is bad, which brings the unhappiness.*

No; it's functional. At this point you're a faker. Look, what you're doing, for instance, is you are creating the feelings that you have. Like say you're at peace and you're resting and somebody says to you, "Why aren't you happy?" Implying you should be happy. What do you believe about the question?

Questioner: *I'd say I believe that yeah, I should be excited and I'm not.*

No; what do you believe about the question? In other words, you believe that's a good question.

Questioner: *It's hypothetical, but yeah, let's say I believe it's a good question.*

You agree with them that you should be happier. Why do you believe that you were not happy if you were at peace?

Questioner: *'Cause I'm believing their definition.*

It's the dare, that's all. Why aren't you like me? I'm the way to be.

What *he* loves is probably being left alone. So then all you've done is you've chosen to believe somebody that you are indeed unhappy. You're not even looking at your own experience, okay? That's what I mean by faking. You don't even have the experience of being unhappy. Well, you say, you are, you agree that you are, even though you're not. That's faking.

Questioner: *Yeah; so I'm lying to myself.*

No; you're lying, yeah; period. To God, too, I suppose. You're not unhappy. You know you're not unhappy. So someone says to you you're unhappy and you say, "Oh, I didn't know that." You're goddamn right you didn't know that. That's functional unhappiness.

But still you're lying. You aren't unhappy. You didn't tell the truth. They said, "Aren't you unhappy?" Your answer truly should be "No" if it's going to be a true answer. Okay. So that's what I meant by lying. You're faking.

Now you've created a problem that only you can undo, which is true about all unhappiness anyway, but you have to undo this differently. You have to just start admitting the truth.

SECTION V

Common Descriptions of Unhappiness

"Needs"

PEOPLE believe they "need" things in order to be happy because they believe they will be caused to be unhappy without them. But unhappiness was merely believing in the first place that it would be wrong to be happy without those needed things. Continuing to be unhappy or fearing becoming unhappy is just denying that that belief "caused" the way they felt.

They are still believing it would have been wrong to have been happy and therefore are going to continue to deny that they were merely acting on that belief. To do otherwise would be to admit that they were really unaffected emotionally but were only believing that that was wrong. We are afraid to admit that we don't "need," as if simple desire alone had no right to be sincere. All the subsequent unhappiness or fears of it is in order to deny that they could actually be so wrong or bad as to have remained happy. They then search for the conditions where it might not be wrong to regain or insure happiness. This is called "trying to get what we need."

Fulfilling a need *is,* therefore, the creating of the condition for making it unnecessary to deny that you are happy. Because when needs are fulfilled it will not be wrong to be happy.

"Wrong"

"WRONG" is a model word meant to be equivalent to any concept that means bad, crazy, contradictory, insincere, lying, immoral, inappropriate, undeserving, no right to be, unworthy, sinful. All these ideas mean "bad for you to be happy." The implication is that you will be more unhappy later if you're not unhappy now (because you are not being the way you should—unhappy). But that only repeats the imperative that you not be happy in the future after being happy now, when you should not have been.

The Essential Characteristics
of Emotional Events

THINGS to be happy about: Things that "prove" we are good for ourselves, or whatever takes away what "proves" we are bad for ourselves (even good luck).

Things to be unhappy about: Things that "prove" we are bad for ourselves, or whatever takes away what "proves" we are good for ourselves (even bad luck).

The things that can matter to happiness or unhappiness can be anything: thoughts or lack of thoughts, remembering or forgetting, desires or lack of certain desires, behavior or lack of behavior, events that happen to or are caused by self, by another person, by nature or God, or by the lack of another person, or loss of a thing. In fact, anything that "means" whether we are good or bad for ourselves.

To believe in sin is to fundamentally believe that I am against my very self, my very good, my own future. Unhappiness is just a secularized belief in sinfulness, wrongness, and is the same as believing that we choose what we know to be wrong or bad for us.

Like Adam and Eve we believe we know that some of what we are happy to choose is actually bad for our happiness. The truth is, though, that the mistakes we may make (if they are) are results of the choices we make *for* what we want, and need not prove we can choose *against* what we want. We need knowledge or better information (if anything), not a change of heart. Our motivation is the best possible human motivation. Given human equipment, we want with human minds and hearts—with human brains and guts. We perceive and choose accordingly with human sensibilities, and only pay with what we have been given to pay with—things we do not need for happiness. There is nothing wrong with the way we work.

To get or keep what we want, even our lives, we need what it takes to do that. Sometimes it seems beyond our capabilities. That perception (whether true or not) is a function of our happiness and intransigent self-interest. Everything that is truly us is an aspect of our happy self-interest, and nothing is not. Our motivation is our self, and identical to our very being. If things do not go the way we want it is not for the lack of our wanting them to, and therefore not from a lack of our best informed motivation.

Good and Bad, or Holy and Evil, when used in a general or moral sense (without an object such as good *to* or good *for* something or goal, or bad *to* or bad for something or purpose), means good or bad for happiness. A good work is one that promotes happiness. A good experience is one that promotes or causes happiness. A good or holy person is one that causes and/or deserves happiness. Conversely, a bad or evil work, or deed, or event is one that causes unhappiness. A bad or evil person is one that causes and deserves unhappiness.

We know from all the above that there simply is no such thing or no one that is bad, evil or unhappy-causing. Nothing can prove that you are bad for you.

SECTION VI

Happiness and Others

Forms of Love

Monday Night Study Group, 1973

I Cannot Help Someone Be Happier

The theme for my talk tonight is the freedom to be happy, and all freedoms that implies: for instance the freedom that we have in being happy, the freedom that we have in wanting others to be happy, the freedom we have in letting others be happy, the freedom that we have in letting others be unhappy, etc.

The basic attitude of The Option Method guide, therapist, or practitioner is to realize that I have no responsibility for the unhappiness of my client. That's essential, and is also one of the biggest hang-ups that helpers often face. I'm here only as a servant to do what I can. For whatever reason I may not help someone become happier, the worst that I have done is to leave them wherever they choose to be.

If they choose to be unhappy, they chose to be unhappy before they came to be with me. They may even choose to be more unhappy while they are with me. That is their right, their freedom. They do not have to be happier for my sake. If I want somebody to be happier for my sake, it will be me—*I* will be happier for my sake. I do not have to be happy for their sake. If they want somebody to be happy for their sake, it could be them—*they* can be happy for their own sake. Everything that they do is for their sake, and that cannot change. Everything I may do is for my sake in some way.

We meet each other with our own personal beliefs and the desires that go with those beliefs. They're ours. We may change them, but each of us changes them for ourselves for our *own* sake. If they are happier after being with me it is because they chose to be happier. Their happiness is totally of their own creation. They do whatever they do for their sakes, not mine.

Love Is Being Happy

Love is being happy. I'm loving you if I'm happy with you. Love, though, is what I'm doing for me: I'm being happy. Love is so universally admired and approved of and feels so basically good because when someone is loving another they're not presenting them with an event that the other feels they must be unhappy about. Somehow we feel we're loved because the person who is loving us is just not presenting us with things that we feel we have to be unhappy about.

After people are like that with us, then it is possible to be happy with all the other presented events they give to us. So in a loving relationship we find that we're not unhappy about what they present to us, which then leaves us free to be happy and happier about what is presented to us. Then it's possible for them to be open to *your* presence.

Love as Protection

Often it is called love when the lover removes the event that the beloved believes they must be unhappy about. Sometimes it is seen as a role of the therapist, or *the* role of a therapist, to love. And sometimes it's seen as a function of loving to take away the thing that the person is unhappy about. That kind of loving is protective.

If you're afraid of spiders, the protective lover will go around killing all the spiders. Whatever it is that you're unhappy about, they'll take it away. If I'm unhappy about your drinking, "if you love me you'll stop drinking" might be a way of doing that.

This is usually the romantic ideal of a lover: a servant protector of needs and fears, like a knight. It's often called love when somebody just protects and serves the needs and fears of another person. In this kind of relationship it is also called love when a lover presents tokens that represent that original serving, protecting, need-fear relationship. For instance if a lover gives candy, flowers, or other non-practical special gifts, it affirms to the beloved that the lover wants them to be happy and is willing to protect and serve even when it only seems like whimsy on the beloved's part. "You have no need for flowers really but I'll love you, I'll give them to you. You have no need for candy. These things are not practical and I'm trying to show you by giving you impractical things that I'll protect you and I'll be with you and I'll care for you even when there are things that I don't value, even when they're just whimsy on your part."

In this relationship the most loving lover would be the one who would tolerate the silliest fears and protect the beloved from their most self-defeating behavior. A woman says, "Oh, I just can't stand that," and he says, "Oh, don't worry, dear, I'll take care of it," no matter how silly he may think it is, that makes him a lover, and the more silly she may get the more protective he seems especially if he starts protecting her from things that he knows that she wouldn't ever have to really be afraid of.

A lover would protect even from things that he saw no need for someone to be protected from—this is the medieval romantic ideal. They might even make up and invent challenges and trysts and searches in order to prove one's love even when they're not there, just to show that they'd be ready in case they were. And so the romantic knight might very well go fight another man just simply because that other man was there to fight, and say he was doing it for his beloved. Do all kinds of things—maybe climb a high mountain and come back with a flower, and he'll go through many trials and tests and challenges.

Love as Giving

We have a modern counterpart to that too, and it's still called love. In this kind of relationship it is also called love when the lover gives presents that not only remove the original fear and need, but also extend that removal to a great emotional distance. Remember we said it was loving if we take away the things that the lover is afraid of. Well, now we not only take them away, but we start giving presents and gifts that symbolize that taking away and show that the fears are even further away, and there is even less reason to be afraid. So for instance, if the beloved fears poverty, the lover would give the beloved more and more substantial safeguards and proofs of their distance from poverty: for instance a house, a second car, a maid, insurance, anything that would then remove the beloved further and further away from the thing they feared. They would all be seen as gifts and presents, and proof of love.

Although these presents may serve the lover's needs, they are presented basically though as being for the beloved. "Here's a new refrigerator, dear, for *your* kitchen." Now it sounds like I don't even eat. The whole idea being, it's got to be for that *other* person, even though *I* would like a new refrigerator in my kitchen or in our kitchen.

Often a present is valued only in proportion to its lack of value to the presenter. If you valued it very much, the person you were giving it to would not value it as much, and would not see it as much of a gift, as if the husband said on a Sunday afternoon, after he washed the car, "I washed the car for you, dear," and she never even drives it. Somehow she wouldn't feel that was a present. In this kind of a relationship the gift would have to be seen as not being for the lover but for the beloved. Let's say if she were constantly complaining about the kind of ties he wears, and then she went and bought him a new tie that she liked and she said, "Now here's a nice tie for you." He's liable to feel that that's not much of a gift; in fact he may even resent it because she values the gift too much.

So when the presenter values the gifts, it proportionately takes away from its value as a love token. And this relationship, it's also called love when the lover gives sexual pleasure to the beloved without regard to their own pleasure. Often if it seems that the lover values the activity more than the beloved, then the beloved may even resent the gift in proportion to the value for the giver. These are the two factors: a present is valued in proportion to its lack of value to the presenter, and resented in proportion to the value for the presenter.

I have not found any relationship based on this that hasn't had sexual problems involved in it; because if for one reason or another one of the partners in a sexual relationship just isn't turned on they will start to resent that the other one is turned on. They start to feel that they're being used: "He or she values sexual activity more than I do."

This kind of love's greatest test is when the beloved needs something contrary to the lover's need, which may be most of the time. This love has sacrifice, duty, responsibility, disappointment, selfishness, etc. in its vocabulary.

Love as Not Being Unhappy

This unhappy fear-need-love is sometimes changed into a happy, wanting love where the lover wants to give the gift of self and wants to help the beloved to enjoy that gift more fully. This lover will desire to protect and serve the beloved's happiness, not only by removing the bad but by helping the beloved to stop fearing and being unhappy with the bad, the not desirable. This lover will help the beloved to be happy not only by giving the good things but by helping the beloved to be more and more open with the good things and the desirable things. And we define good and bad as: "bad" are those non-desirable things and "good" are those desirable things.

This lover is happy with the beloved's loving behavior and not unhappy with the non-loving behavior. Not threatened, not scared, not frightened. This lover is happy with the beloved's hopes and not unhappy with their fears. This love may not have any vocabulary.

Love in a Therapeutic Relationship

Now this is the kind of love an Option Method guide will have for his or her clients. Because I love my clients I will not pretend that their unhappiness is not theirs, and that they need to be protected from the things that they're unhappy about. I will not bail them out by giving them what they believe they have to have from me before they will allow themselves to be happy with me. Since I love them, I will not pretend to save them. I will not pretend that they are not totally responsible for their judgments, their beliefs, and their concomitant emotions. If they hate me for being who I am, I will not hate them by pretending that I am responsible for their self-imposed hate. It is not love to help another believe that they are helpless. It's not love to help another believe that their happiness depends on who I am and how I behave.

If I do not think of the right questions to ask them in our sessions, it's not their fault in any way, but neither is it my fault if their unhappiness and happiness depend on my questions. If I'm blocked, if I've forgotten, if I'm distracted, if I'm confused, if I'm unclear, it's not their fault regardless of how they may have acted. But neither is it my fault or my responsibility in any way if their happiness depends on my questions. I did not set up their lives so that their happiness has to depend on my questions.

This is the therapist's freedom to not do therapy. If I love them, I will not play games to satisfy their demands. I will give them absolutely nothing on the basis of that they're unhappy with my not giving them what they want. If they're unhappy with my not giving them something, I'm not going to give it to them *just* because they're unhappy with not having it. Maybe I'll give it to them, maybe

I won't, but their unhappiness won't be my reason. Perhaps I'll be the first person in their lives to not be afraid of their threats against themselves to make themselves unhappy if I don't do what they want.

It is not love to show them that their unhappiness pays off, that their unhappiness with me gets them what they want. If on the other hand I do give them what they want it will be in spite of their unhappiness, and if they want to believe I've given in to their threats, so be it. I'm not obliged to give them what they demand, nor am I obliged to not give them what they demand. I'm totally free, and I will be totally free. That is loving them. I do what I wish; they will behave as they wish.

I'm loving my clients by giving them only exactly, no more, no less, than what I'm happy to give. In time they may realize that they are really being loved. They will know that when I am giving something it is truly, freely, happily given and that whatever I do give there is no resentment behind it. And so then they will know that I could never resent their asking or demanding for what I don't give since I am freely and happily also refusing to give and not give it. If I am happy they may know that they're loved; *I* know that they're loved.

I'm an Option Method guide because people who want me to help them to be happier motivate me to do that. I'm a guide or a therapist to some people and not for others because those for whom I am a therapist are the ones who have motivated me to be that way for them.

The difference between being an Option Method practitioner *and* lover, and a lover in other relationships is simple: essentially there's no real difference. I love and I'm happy with everybody. Some motivate me to be with them in some ways, others in other ways, and still others not at all. I love or I'm happy with all. In an Option Method session I am the lover by helping the other to be happy. In what we might call a mutually loving relationship I am also the beloved and am being helped to be happier.

In The Option Method session I agree to not seek help from this person but only to help and that in form or in style would be the *only* difference, and so that the difference between a professional or an unprofessional relationship is that in friendships I'm motivated by whatever there is in that friend, in that person to be with them for whatever there is to be with them. I will help them, they will help me. I will love them, they will love me. I am the beloved as well as the lover to one degree or another. In the session I ask none of that from my client. I do not ask them to love me, I do not ask them to be happy with me, which is something I might ask from my friends. I do not ask them to understand me, appreciate me, applaud me, hug me, or to do anything for me that helps me to be happy with them. I do not ask them to do anything that has to do exactly with that lover-beloved relationship.

A professional session is one where I ask for something other than love in return for my help. And that's perhaps what makes all "business," or professions and their relationships, other than friendship relationship. When I go to the butcher he doesn't ask me for my love, I don't ask him for his love. I ask him for his meat, he asks me for my money, and that's it. We're not asking for love from one another. In this relationship I am being asked for love but I'm not asking for it in return.

In each I am happy; in each I try to help the other to be happy. In each I may receive many things I want. In the therapeutic relationship I am only wanted for one particular skill or task. In other relationships, I may be wanted for other abilities, other qualities of mine. What makes the professional relationship *professional* is the desire of the seeker, the desire of the client, the desire of the petitioner, of the beloved. All they want from me is my skill. All they ask of me is that task. They want to use me that way, so that is going to delineate, perhaps, the relationship. It's not so much that I'm going to approach it differently but that the client is basically approaching it differently.

To Love Is to Be Happy and
Do What You Want

B E with. Don't be with.
Smile. Don't smile.
Be loving. Don't be loving.
Be affectionate. Don't be affectionate.
Give or say what you want. Take or ask for what you want.
Do your own thing.

If the one you love gets unhappy, it's not because you are not loving them enough. Their happiness does not depend on you. If you find you want them to be happy, it is because you want it. It's not because you are a loving person or feel the need to prove to them that you are loving.

You are loving if you are happy. You will be loving if you are not afraid.

If you are happy with someone in order to be a nice, loving person, then your happiness will depend on them seeing you as loving. Every time you don't feel particularly loving or giving, you will feel like a failure as a lover. Every time they don't act loving and they don't give you what you ask, you will also feel like a failure as a lover.

When you feel like a failure, guilty, ungiving, and unfeeling, you will need to run away. You will be repulsed by your lover and play right into their fear of failure. If you believe you are a failure because you are not able to accept what is offered to you, or because you find that you are not able to get the kind of love you want, you will then be over-attracted to your lover, playing right into their fear of failure again.

This kind of view of being a lover is really worth failing at. You only fail to love if you get unhappy. In this kind of relationship you only get unhappy because you believe you failed to love. If you don't feel or do something that prevents your lover from being unhappy you are not failing to love.

You fail to love if you get unhappy about it.

You fail to love if you are afraid of your lover being unhappy.

If you want evidence that you are a loving person, you will only find it in your happiness. If you are happy, you are loving everyone. When you are happy, you are glad for everyone's happiness.

A lover is not someone you are more happy with. A lover is someone you are with happily. When you are happy, you will want more things with some people than others. When you are happy, you will want to give to some people more than others. If a lover is different or special, it is because you are both wanting very much together.

With a lover you are glad for everything they do when they are happy. You may find that if you are not so glad, it is because they are not so happy and are not especially doing what they want. You are aware of any fear in them and loss of happiness. You know each other perfectly in the sense that you are as aware of their gladness and happiness as you are of your own. This experience is not because you are afraid of their unhappiness, but because you want them to be happy. You love them and want the gladness you will both have when they are happier. A lover is someone you want to be glad with together.

Lovers are two people who come together to learn how not to be unhappy and who look forward to more gladness together. They come together not to learn how to be loving to someone, but to grow in happiness. You want to see happiness and gladness in them and you want them to see and experience it in you. You want to help each other have more happiness and less fear. The only way to help create this is to be happy yourself and to do what you want. Don't be unhappy about their unhappiness.

Problems and games set in after one gets unhappy either with themselves or you. They usually experience it as failing to love you and resent your desiring something that they are afraid of failing at. This fear of failing at being loving makes them more concerned with looking loving than being happy. They feel tested by you. They are quick to believe and imagine that they are hurting you by not giving or doing what they believe you want. They don't realize that no matter what you may have wanted, you certainly didn't want them to be unhappy.

The games begin if you believe that you have not been loving enough or that you can overcome their unhappiness by being more loving yourself. Then you try to be extra loving, understanding, forgiving, and eager to fix things to show how loving you are. That will turn them off more. You are now both afraid of being unloving. Now you are being loving in order to get them to love you. You feel you simply want them to be happy, but in fact, you are needing them to be happy so that they will show how loving you can be. You even hope to inspire them to be loving. You both want to achieve what is the cause of the problem, lovingness.

Real love is to be happy and to just want them to be happy. You make your choice. Do you want to be happy and love or do you want to be loving instead? The difference is a choice of intention. The behavior may be the same but the motivation is vastly different. Motivated by fear, you will merely be loving your lovingness.

A lover is someone with whom you don't have to be loving in order to get what you want.

When your lover does not accept what you offer, just let yourself know that you do what you want. Do not be unhappy because it seems that you were wrong. Don't demand that they take what you offer in order to be nice and loving toward you. Don't demand acceptance. Don't demand that they be happy. Do not test yourself to see if you are unloving or unhappy.

Unhappy loving is being nice when you don't really feel like it and doing what you don't want really want to do. You feel conflicted or split because it is obvious that sometimes unhappy people will want proof of your love. If you are more concerned with appearing loving, you will either do what they want without feeling like it, feeling resentful, or you will be turned off and refuse even if you really want to do it.

Being happy is something you can do for someone, even if they need it as proof of your love, but do it as a conscious choice. If you get unhappy about their unhappiness, your motivations will be unclear. You are always unhappy every time you hold to the belief that you should get love by being loving or that you should return love by feeling loving.

Do not be concerned if your lover is not loving. You can know you are happy and love if you are allowed to say yes or no freely and if your lover is allowed to say yes or no to your offers. You love and are happy if you allow another to say no and realize they do not have to accept your gift.

Our real desire is not to succeed or fail at being lovers or teachers or students or friends, but just to be happy. I do not fail you if you or I fail to be happy. You do not fail me if you or I are unhappy. I can be happy because I can be and want to be. You can be happy because you can be and want to be.

On Fervor

THE realization, or even the suspicion, that we may not be serving our desires by exposing them to others does not mean we must be believing that they are wrong or dangerous in themselves. The issues of privacy, protection and a better means of attainment may be more to the point. To be an object of ridicule may or may not be useful in our lives. We may decide on that basis how we can achieve our goals, whatever they may be.

We may not be expressing to the world what we know about happiness. We may have decided to be more private. That does not mean we are afraid, or are actually against happiness in our lives. We may not have the praise of others for our happiness, or even the simple agreement that it is desirable to be happy. So what? Happiness is personal, only personal, intrinsically personal. What would the approval or "sharing" of happiness with others do for us or them? Nothing. At most it is our self-expression in the presence of another. There can be no true sharing in the sense that a portion of our happiness can be experienced by others as their happiness.

Rather than lose our fervor for want of camaraderie, we can look to ourselves as sources of inspiration and affirmation. We know we do not need this, but we may still know that it is for us to still want it, and enjoy doing it. Are you allowed to affirm what you know?

The one thing necessary for your happiness is for you to know (or experience) your own happiness.

SECTION VII

Option as Therapy

To Have Happiness Nothing Is Necessary

June 22, 1992

UNHAPPINESS is, itself, believing that something is necessary. Only not believing in the necessity of unhappiness is necessary. In that sense only one thing is necessary; which is the same as realizing that nothing is necessary.

To have happiness there is only one thing necessary: to have happiness. It is self-defined.

To have joy there is only one thing necessary: to have joy. Joy is being glad to be happy. Being glad to be happy is to admit that you are.

It is not necessary to deny in any way that you are. You may gladly deny it to others, of course, if you wish, but you never have to believe that you are wrong to continuously appreciate yourself, and your wisdom in happiness.

I knew a man who had a tremendous, paralyzing and sickening fear of flying in airplanes. He, of course, believed he deserved to fall from a great height. He believed that if he flew when he shouldn't, he would certainly fall. Panic was, for him, a necessity.

This same man noticed he had a sexual attraction to his teenage step-daughter who was developing, nubile, and affectionate. He dared to contemplate the great heights of sexual ecstasy that would ensue from engaging in this forbidden delight. He, of course, believed he needed to be prevented, or else fall from that great height. Panic was, for him, a necessity.

When I questioned what he feared about his attraction he disclosed that although she would welcome his intimacy now, that in the future when she socialized more and accepted the normal beliefs of others she would believe she should turn against him and accuse him of harming her. He was afraid he would be overwhelmed by attraction, nevertheless, and get in trouble. He believed that if he flew when he shouldn't, he would certainly fall.

I asked him, considering what he believed about her future actions, if he thought that acting on his attractions would be good for him. He said that he believed such an involvement, although pleasant at first, would be harmful to him later.

I asked him if, that being the case, is he still sexually attracted to her. He said no. He said that there is no longer any attraction when he realizes what it really means to his welfare.

"So," I asked, "do you need to fight or fear your attraction?"

"There is no attraction to what is bad for me. No problem. I thought I had to fight the initial attraction when, in fact, I really don't have any attraction when I consider my total feelings."

I asked, "By the way, how do you feel about flying?"

His eyes lit up. "I don't feel any fear. It's like it was miraculously removed," he said.

The Right to Be Happy

January 26, 1991

ALL people are allowed to be happy at all times, forever. This is happiness; to know you are always allowed to be happy no matter who you are, what you do and no matter what happens to you.

All people have the right to be happy. It is never wrong to be happy. Those who know it are happy forever.

Blessed are those who know they are happy.

Happy are those who know they are blessed.

To be blessed is to have the right to be happy. To be born is to be allowed to be happy. To know you are allowed to be happy is to be blessed.

Happiness is being allowed to be happy.

Happiness is not believing it is wrong to be happy.

Happiness is not believing it will become wrong to be happy.

Happiness is not fearing you will have no right to be happy.

Happiness is not believing you should be unhappy.

Happiness is not believing you have to be unhappy.

Happiness is not believing it is right to be unhappy.

It is evident. God permits you to be happy no matter what or when. Nature permits you to be happy no matter what or when. The only permission you need is yours to be happy all the time.

You don't have to deny your happiness ever. It is not wrong to be happy always. It is merely believed to be wrong.

SECTION VIII

Myths of the "Ideal" Way of Being

The Myth of Mental Illness

O PTION Therapy has a point of view that distinguishes it from other therapies. Part of that point of view is that mental illness is seen as a social myth, and that it does not actually exist in any of the ways that we could use the term "illness," or "mental illness."

You see, when people used to behave differently from other people it never made any difference to anyone except that they bothered them, and if this was two, three, four thousand years ago if you "bothered" somebody you got punished for it, or punished in some way, depending on how many people you bothered. If you bothered the community you were considered a renegade or an outlaw or something like that, usually expelled from the community or punished within the community. It was considered a strictly social, cultural means of achieving normality for the community, called harmony, peace, or law and order—whatever you want. And it seemed that there were people that would respond to these kinds of treatment in ancient times, and after they were punished or ostracized, they would come around to the social norms of behavior.

Now there were those people who would never come around, and they were a problem because that meant that this system of getting people to conform was not working, and after they tried everything, perhaps they would kill them. But if killing just did not fit into the other taboos of the culture, and the way the person bothered people was not that severe, was not that serious, they said that he was possessed by an evil spirit. So, "possession by an evil spirit" was a term to describe somebody whose non-conformity was not bad enough to be killed, whose non-conformity was so consistent that punishment did not make any difference. After a while, in fact, in some cultures and societies it was said that these people were not possessed by evil spirits but by the gods, i.e., "struck mad by the gods." Again, the whole implication being that "We cannot do anything about them, so let us refer to what they do as having come from somewhere other than from this life we know." And, it was a social designation that was what was meant by "madness."

The Greeks had great respect for a mad person. A mad person, again, was a person who would dare to say things and to do things that were not capital offences, remember, and that no amount of punishment would appear to change. Only certain classes of people were allowed to be mad. For instance, if you were a slave and you were mad, that would not be considered from the gods or the devils. You would just be killed. But if you came from a rich family, then you were entitled to be eccentric, which is pretty much the case today.

But in either case, the whole idea of mental illness has its social implications from the very beginning. Somewhere along the line—now this continued, by the way, all the way through the Middle Ages—it was attributed to various things, usually sin. Apparently in Roman times it was believed to be evil spirits, and then it was possession by devils, and then later on in the Middle Ages it was considered to still have been devils, but as a result of sin now, perhaps of the sin of the parents. It was due to certain helplessness on the part of society to deal with it, that they had to resort to this terminology.

The mentally ill person was called "crazy," an "animal," whatever, because they could not be made to conform. If their non-conformity was not threatening to the political structure they were called "crazy." If it was threatening to the political structure, they were called "traitors."

It was all right if you thought you were god, as long as you went around ranting and raving on the streets. But if you still thought you were god and gathered around you a small group of followers and plotted to overthrow the government, to enthrone you and install you in your godhead—well, that was a little different. Nobody could afford that kind of craziness. By political designation that man was not called insane, but he was called rebellious. By and large such people were locked up and put away.

Along came a movement called "Psychoanalysis" that said "Hey, maybe it has nothing to do with devils or evil spirits. Maybe it has to do with our own attitudes toward these people. Maybe it has to do with their attitudes toward themselves. Maybe this is very much a human problem. Maybe it very much has human causes."

And Freud and his followers began to investigate so-called "madness" and they gave it a new dimension. They said: "This is not evil. It is something else. It is 'sick,' and we should not look at these people as evil any more. We have to make a great step forward in humanity and view these people as sick." What is happening today with drug addiction, with alcoholism, it is getting very humane and very "in" to view these people as sick—not rotten.

So, Freud was a physician, his followers were physicians, and when he said "sick" he meant "sick." He meant "sick" just like cancer, just like a broken leg, just like the common cold. In fact, the neurosis he talked about was as common as the common cold. And he seemed to be very comfortable with that.

But he used a medical model, and at that point in history it would seem to be a great step forward to say that men were no longer evil but that some of them were sick.

But who were the people we were talking about? People who did not behave the way we would like them to. People who bothered us. We still called them something other than people; we still said they were something other than people like ourselves. They were basically people who bothered us, and we changed and traded the word "evil" for the word "sick." And we have gotten rid of the witch doctors and the priests and installed psychoanalysts, psychiatrists. But the so-called "sick people" were still being put in jails, but the name of the jail was changed to "hospital." They were still being tortured, but it was called "therapy." It still is called "electroshock therapy." They used to whip them in the Middle Ages to make them conform, and now they just rack their whole body with electroshock treatment. "I'll get you out of it somehow. I'll snap you out of it."

In the Middle Ages they said it was for your sake because you were going to go to Hell. They still say it is for your sake, because you are crazy and we want you to be sane. They never admitted in the Middle Ages that they wanted these people to conform because they would be more comfortable that way, and they still do not admit it now.

Why do they hunt out these people? Why do they find them? Because they do not conform.

And so what I am coming to say is that the term "mental illness" is a very unscientific one for a number of reasons: it has absolutely nothing to do with science, and it has everything to do with politics.

The word "mental illness" is a political term. It means "people who I am not comfortable with," "people who our society is not comfortable with."

It is unscientific, too, as a conceptual framework because it refers to it as an illness, implying that there is a health, calls it a sickness implying that there is a state of well-being and that we know what that state is and we know what the sickness is.

No one claims how they know, so that along came some people to say "Well, we are trying to cure these sick people but we haven't really been justifying it, so we'll take statistical samplings and we'll establish what we call a "norm." That will give us a little more justification. And so along about 1900 the birth of Psychology as we know it today was meant to justify psychotherapy in many, many ways. If I develop a norm then I can decide who does not fit that norm, and it will have a new religious quality to it. It will have the weight of authority behind it, and I can point out with quite clear decisiveness that these people do not conform. They are "abnormal." Enter the word "abnormal" now, with some real statistical reality.

Illness implies diagnosis, implies pathology. It implies nomenclature. And so we have that today. So somebody comes in, we name the illness, we diagnose it and say it's "paranoid," for example. Then we say "It has three causes, and we can trace the whole history and origin of this disease, and it is really pathological." Then, we can prescribe. We can say "Okay, then a certain course of treatment is necessary." The implications being that a paranoiac is suffering from a disease different from—let us say—an obsessive compulsive is suffering from. Otherwise why would I use the two different terms?

And then the causes and origins of these diseases are different. And of course the method of treatment will of course be different. See, as in medicine and in the other healing arts, you do not treat a headache as you would treat a broken leg. That is what is also implied by psychotherapy. You would not treat paranoia as you would treat obsessive compulsiveness. But nobody ever asked why not. We just accepted the medical model that these were separate diseases and they respond better to certain kinds of treatment. And some respond better to some kinds of treatment than another kind of treatment.

So we went out to prove our case, that there were different diseases with different causes, and they were treated differently. Because we began with that premise that apparently that is what makes the difference. There is no virus, so how can you call it an illness?

When we talk about ourselves as being sick, let us say with a cold, or with a fever, or with whatever, that is something that happened to us, you see. It happened to us. Our bodies were invaded by a virus, or hit by an automobile, or something. But somehow it was something we passively received and for which we were a victim—as in the word "patient," which means "sufferer."

And so we were seen to have suffered some kind of a thing happening to us. That was just accepted in mental illness too. The poor person is suffering from this disease. The word "suffering" was used in the same way that it was used in "suffering from a broken leg," implying that it happened to the person, and then "the disease" implying that there was an external cause again. And of course using the word disease meant external cause, nomenclature, diagnosis, without prescription, all a false justification. It had never been questioned.

And yet, if ever you pinned down a psychotherapist he would say "Yes, of course it comes from the person. It doesn't come from outside. Yes, of course I deal with the patient."

So if the causes (and they are, if it is a disease) are from outside, then no amount of psychotherapy with the individual would help, would it? And if the reason why we are the way we are is because that is the way our mother and father made us, well then it seems to me that we need our mother and father in the therapy session, to remake us and help us be born again and be remade, if it is so true that is what made us the way we are. There is a whole question of not having a choice.

In ancient times a man could not be healed except by the grace of God or the grace of the gods. In later times a man could not be healed unless by the grace of the psychoanalyst. But somehow external intervention was seen as to be necessary and some miracle had to be worked because apparently this was a disease that was inevitable. And yet the admission that there is a therapy is a denial of its inevitability.

Option Therapy is an existential humanistic approach which starts asking questions, and starts with the whole medical model of mental illness is a myth. We are not talking about a virus, you are not talking about anything you can put under a microscope, you are not talking about an illness. You are talking about how people feel, and what they do to themselves. And you are talking about people's behavior and how they act upon themselves. You are talking about how people choose to be. And when you say "illness" you are implying that they did not want to be that way, that they had to be that way. Why should we make that implication without finding out? Why do we decide that all of our so-called crazy people or our so-called normal people are "products?" See, it is a nice battle: are we products of our environment or are we products of our heredity? Not even allowing another possibility, that we are not products at all. That our behavior is not a product of either our environment or of our heredity. That our behavior is what it is because it is what we choose it to be.

Now, if you want to know why *we* choose it to be, that is where Option Psychology comes in. We find that all behavior is chosen. All behavior other than that physical, biological behavior which is the study of the physio-biologist. And that what are commonly called "emotions," or "emotional disturbances," or "emotional states," etc., are very freely and directly chosen by the person who is so-called "suffering" this. The person is not suffering it by any means, in the sense that it happens. They suffer in the sense that they feel bad. But they are not suffering in the sense of the original meaning of the word, which was "suffer something": something happens to me. I am very passive when that happens.

Every person who is very unhappy walks into my office and says things, you know, like "This makes me mad. I hear voices coming into my head. They are doing this to me. They are doing that to me. Everything makes me be what I am. I am pretty much helpless. Elevators make me afraid." This makes me that." Always talking about things "making" them, very much in the sense of their own helplessness, and believing it very much. But that does not make it true, does it, just because they believe it? It would be very unscientific for the doctor to believe you when you walked in and said "I have appendicitis, would you please remove my appendix?" What kind of a physician would that be? But, you walk into the psychoanalyst's office and say "My husband makes me unhappy, would you please remove my husband?" And you will start upon a course of therapy to enable you to get the strength to kick your husband out of the house. But in some sense buying the story that something is happening to you, and that you have got to develop the strength to fight against it, talking about such things as "weak ego, weak self, strong self," all implying that we need strengths that we do not have in order to fight this world that we live in. The world that is constantly grinding us down and making us sick.

Buying the presumption without asking "Is it true?" Just what if it was not true? What if it was not the world that was making us sick, but that it was us that was making ourselves unhappy? Because that's what we were believing, that the world was making us sick, perhaps.

Just what if the paranoiac was not really hearing voices, or was really hearing voices? It is very unscientific to begin with either direction. But to label the person as a paranoiac implies that we really know what is going on. But we do not know what is going on. All that has been happening in psychotherapy and psychoanalysis, more and more, is that we more and more learn that we do not know what is going on. But we act as if we know. We feel very helpless, we feel like neophytes, we feel very courageous and very heroic entering into this unknown, uncharted area of the human mind. It is a lot of baloney.

That we know ourselves is one of the principles of Option Psychology. Knowing that fact is the beginning of entering into the therapeutic relationship between the doctor and the patient. And so the patient comes in and says "Doctor, you tell me what is wrong with me. Doctor, you help me find out what is wrong with me."" And he says, "Yes, we'll search through your history and subconscious and find out those things that are being hidden from you." How could they possibly be "being hidden" from you? Who else is there in your body besides you?

You are hiding them from yourself. But you do not say that to the patient. All right, you might say it after awhile. Then the patient says "Oh, I'm hiding it from myself." How do you know what to hide if you do not know what it is in the first place? If I said to you: "Don't think of the word hippopotamus for the next ten seconds," how many of you could do that without knowing that you are not supposed to think of the word hippopotamus? And so you have to think "Don't think hippopotamus" and already it is too late. "Don't think of what my mother did to me—what? What did she do to me? Oh, yeah. Don't think about . . . oh yeah." And you have to go back and forth thinking about what you are not supposed to be thinking about.

If there is such a thing as repression, suppression, loss of memory, the unconscious, it means knowing what you know and denying it—that's all. It doesn't mean not knowing it. It can't mean not knowing it. If you didn't know it then it couldn't be there, and then you wouldn't know what to repress, suppress, or forget. You knew what to remember when you started this so-called "search." If you didn't know where "hidden" thoughts were in the first place, you found them when you discovered that they were "hidden."

So, there's a complete lack of faith in the patient, and a complete ignorance. Very frequently, the therapist believes the patient doesn't really know what's going on and "I'm going to help them." In Option Therapy we know that that's not true.

And we find this: in examining people, in examining how they are who they are and what they do, we find that everything that they do follows from a belief that they have. And everything that they feel follows from a very real belief. So, that goes for us. Everything we feel and everything we do is based on very, very real beliefs that we have. Our emotional responses are chosen.

The Medical Model of Mental Illness

GROW: December 13, 1971

In the talk "The Medical Model of Mental Illness," Bruce Di Marsico discusses the mythologies behind the medical model of mental illness.

The medical model is the framework of diagnosis and treatment to achieve a healthy state. When used in the psychotherapeutic context, the medical model proposes that there are behavioral or attitudinal pathologies, that there is a healthy state that is free of these pathologies, and that there is a treatment regime to cure the pathologies.

Observing that what is considered pathological in one culture may not be considered pathological in another, he points out that the medical model is a method of imposing social standards. History is full of social standards that *were* considered illnesses, but no longer are. In contemporary times in the West, many sexual behaviors are losing their status as illnesses, for example, homosexuality, nymphomania, and masturbation.

He discusses the goals of therapy. The purpose of therapy is for the patient to be happy, not to achieve any ideal way of being, such as being "well-adjusted." The patient's happiness is whatever it is for them, and the patient is the sole decider of what his or her problem is. When the therapist believes the patient has a problem, and the patient does not, this is usually because the therapist is finding the patient's attitude or behavior is a reason for their own (the therapist's) unhappiness. This is the therapist's issue, not the patient's.

NOTHING mental inherently falls under my rejection of a medical model. For example, insofar as a particular type of schizophrenia may be a medical problem, it's a medical problem.

What does the medical model hypothesize in terms of mental illness? It becomes a medical model simply because it is using the word "illness" to start with. Making a description of behavior is one thing, but if you say there is pathology behind it, you are saying something quite a bit different.

The medical model is what most psychotherapy begins with; again, we're not talking about what is treated medically; we're talking only about what is treated psychotherapeutically. Now what do we mean by using the medical model with the psychotherapeutic technique? *Is* there a question of pathology that we're trying to deal with? What does it mean to diagnose a "problem"?

Anyone going to a therapist conceives themselves of having a problem. That's why they went to a therapist. If they conceive of themselves with a problem and if they don't go to a therapist, you don't have to worry about treating them. We're not discussing involuntary patients here, such as those in the criminal justice system.

If I am a patient, if you want to deal with me, then you have to deal with *my* reality. To make the judgment that my reality is not real is less than useless. It's hardly the point that a patient and a therapist don't see things the same way. So if you say that you, as a therapist, see a problem and the patient doesn't, and the patient seems to be bringing up another problem, what problem do you, as a therapist, see that the patient doesn't see? The question is, is the patient happy or not? If you think the patient's unhappy about something, and he disagrees, that is merely a difference of opinion, and their opinion is more relevant than yours in this context.

There is a question of imposing social standards of behavior. What is the purpose of psychotherapy? To change somebody into what *we* want them to be? When you use a medical model, you talk about changing someone according to a standard. Can you call it "helping" if you're helping someone against their will? To do what they don't want to do? For their own good? The greatest evils that have ever befallen mankind have been for people's "own good." It is a line that every dictator has ever taken; any senator who doesn't vote the way his constituency wants, is still voting "for their own good," he says.

The whole question of what you do for other people's own good has to be solved for the psychotherapist. What is it that you're after when you have a patient? What is it that you want really? What are you hoping to do?

If you start peeling away all your motives, like an onion, you get down to "to get happy." Now, what frequently happens with the medical model, is that the goal is that the patient will be adjusted into "well adapted," a good fit into the social strata, functional.

But why do I, as a therapist, want this for you? What's unspoken is that what I want to do is help you to be happy, and because it's not spoken very frequently we find ourselves mouthing such things as "The fact that you're happy or not is immaterial, you're not adjusted." The whole purpose of setting up a medical model or any other model was to achieve the patient's happiness, and certainly we get into this field to achieve our own happiness. Now what can disturb us sometimes is if the patient's happiness is antagonistic to our own happiness, if the patient's happiness is threatening to our own happiness.

That's why some therapists will have this attitude: they become frightened and say, "Well, I'm working for your happiness, but you might want to do some things that I'm not so happy about, so therefore let's revert to a standard that the majority of us will be happy with, and that I feel I'll be happy with, and if I can't make myself be happy with it, I'll *make* myself be happy with it, and if you can't make yourself be happy with it, let's have a norm." And from this comes the emergence of a norm, a happy medium. The word "norm" practically means compromise in almost every sense of the word: you lower your expectations; I'll raise mine, and let's try to adjust and cope, and try to be happy with that.

But again, behind it all is "And let's try to be happy." So behind any course of therapy, or any reason to be going to therapy, is to be happy. Why would a patient come to you in the first place except to be happy?

There is still something inside you, something you want, something you're striving for, something you won't be content without, and that's behind everything else, and why you *do* everything else. I'm using the term "happiness" for convenience, to give that a convenient term that we can somewhat all identify with. It's a compromise norm to use that word. But there is that in us that whatever you're after, you will see that there is a chain of motives, and as you go back the reason why you're doing anything is in order to be happy. There isn't a single possible action that you could perform that you weren't performing in order to be happy. There isn't a single thing that you would do that wasn't to be happy, however you define happiness.

You couldn't possibly act against what you believe happiness is. Even if you're unhappy, you're unhappy in order to be happy.

Everyone is utterly free, and the kind of behavior that we manifest is not the result of underlying pathology but the result of certain beliefs, and sometimes the ways that we believe that we can be happy are just mistaken.

There are some of you here that don't feel that you choose your feelings. If you are rejected by someone that you love, you really love and want to love you, you'll often say, "I feel terrible," "I feel bad," or "I feel sad and unhappy that this person rejected me," "They made me feel bad." And we often talk like that, as if the other person's behavior made us have a certain feeling. We speak about it as if unhappiness were a medical thing, as if it were a virus transmitted that caused us to feel a certain way, that their words made us feel this, that being rejected made us feel unhappy. Now what I ask you is this: if you look at it, if you had the choice to feel any way you wanted to feel, how many of you would have chosen to feel differently anyway? How many of you *want* to feel happy if someone you love rejects you?

Why assume that something *makes* you happy, as if something happened to you? You may not be aware of what you are doing but you are making a choice to be happy.

You also make a choice to assimilate someone else's goals. There are people who grow up in the same family, with the same parents, who don't assimilate their parent's goals while their sisters or brothers may very well do so, and somewhere those people made a choice. One chose to assimilate, and the other chose not to. Now whether they are going to be happy as a consequence of this choice is another matter, but it was a *choice*. You may have no choice about circumstances, but what you do choose is how you feel about them and what you do about them. You're never prevented from choosing to be happy; you just don't want to do so.

Sometimes people talk as if conditioning is not a choice, but conditioning is the recognition that something is good for you and you're going to continue to take it as long as it is good, or that a thing is bad for you and you're going to continue to avoid it as long as you see it as bad.

If you place yourself in a situation, say that someone you loved died and you had the absolute choice, and if you could choose to be happy or unhappy, what would you choose? Let's say that you choose to be unhappy, well that's what you would choose. And that's the way you would feel. If you find that your feelings exactly coincide with what you want to feel, what's the sense of complaining about not having free choice then? And that's what we're trying to see, because the greatest complaint of every patient who comes to you is "Doctor, I'm feeling what I don't want to feel."

This person feels they would be terribly unhappy if they chose to be happy. That's why he's choosing to be unhappy. It is unthinkable to him: that he could be happy after suffering such a great loss. He only knows that "I've loved so well, I've loved so much and now I'm losing so much" He only sees a tremendous loss for himself. Seeing loss and seeing the harm to himself that's going to come from it, can he willingly welcome something that he sees is "bad" for him? So once he's perceived what is bad for him, he's not going to be happy with it, he's not going to welcome it. But in those societies where they see this as something good both for the person who dies and the people who are left behind, societies that propose that these people become saints and can intercede for you in the spirit realm, and benefit you, you have happiness for parallel reasons. It depends on how you view the event.

We make these choices on how to view events, and what is behind them and why do we make them? What's behind them is our view of whether a thing is good or bad for us, whether it fosters our happiness or not.

We find that we make a judgment on everything that we see, and the belief is usually fundamental: that this is good for me or bad for me. It's kind of primitive: if we believe that a thing is bad for us, we'll never choose it; if we believe it's good for us, we'll gladly choose it, we'll really enjoy it and somehow that's got a lot to do with being happy or not, if what we see is good or bad for us.

A patient comes in and is very unhappy. He is manifesting his unhappiness in all kinds of ways: he's a manic-depressive, a paranoiac, using these labels. If you understand that these labels are descriptions of the way he's acting out his unhappiness, then you're looking at it differently and you have something to start with. He's choosing to behave this way. Why is it that we can't see so clearly what we've known for so long, that our systems of neuroses and psychoses are so cultural? They always take certain forms. When people act out in this country they act out in a certain way, within certain well-defined limits. When a berserker goes berserk, he gets his hatchet and he runs around cutting off people's heads. That just doesn't happen in the United States. Various so-called neuroses and sicknesses are just as well learned as any other form of behavior. What we're concerned with is not that the manifestation implies a pathology, but that it implies an *unhappiness*, and if the unhappiness were not there, neither would the self-defeating behavior.

Those therapists or religious figures who propose an ideal way of being, are saying that the patient's behavior is not a way that they will be happy with. They have the impulse to say, "Behave as you should, damn you!," because they are searching for their own happiness, wanting everyone else to behave, and so they come up with the ways of behavior that they need the patient to manifest in order to be happy with them, and that they feel the rest of us would need to be happy with, "if we would only face it."

The Option Therapist point of view is, "If it made you unhappy enough you wouldn't do it, but you're choosing to do it because you believe that in the long run you're going to be happier for it. Now you may be mistaken, so let's look at why you believe these things and see if your beliefs are valid or not, whether the beliefs are myths." This is not a rhetorical question. There is no presumption that the beliefs are valid or not.

Let's look at some examples of myths of mental illness.

Take those who are suicidal. If you're an Option Therapist what you will hear them say is that "I choose to live but I also choose to be unhappy with it." See, the problem is not in choosing not to live, the problem is in deciding and swearing and promising to be unhappy if you live. It comes from the belief that you can't really be happy. And that's a very real belief for that person.

And consider a person who hears voices. The Option Therapist does not seek to "cure" the voices; "cure" is a medical term. In Option Therapy, the voices may stop, but then again, they may do something else. The point is for the patient to not have to be *afraid* of their feelings about the voices. And the voices may disappear or not, that isn't an issue.

Or consider a patient I had who was afraid of being a "nymphomaniac." The issue here is not whether nymphomania is a valid term. By "nymphomania," she meant, "a way I don't want to be." What you do is just ask them, why does she believe that if she has these feelings she will become a nymphomaniac, does she have any good reason to believe it? And she might think about it and say, "No, I just always have believed it. The only reason that I have is that I always have. But I have no reason at all."

And then the further revelation, "You mean that I don't have to believe that? I can have my own feelings? I don't have to be a nymphomaniac if I don't want to?" She's going to be a nymphomaniac against her will?

You don't convince them of anything. The person just eventually begins to see that their own choices were so self-defeating that they don't need them anymore: their choices didn't get them what they wanted. What she wanted was protection against being a nymphomaniac and she didn't need protection, and she came to realize that. It was the recognition that she wouldn't be happy as a nymphomaniac that set up this whole thing in the first place. And the only protection she ever needed from being a nymphomaniac was just not wanting to be one.

On Perfectionism
January 19, 1992

THERE are people who believe they have to blame themselves and feel bad when they are the practical cause of something they didn't want occurring. The whole point is to not feel bad about that.

You get in a car without checking your tires—and one of them is bald. You may say "What did I do wrong? Why does this happen to me?" We have a part to play in what happens to us sometimes, but we don't have to put ourselves on trial to declare ourselves innocent by cause of simply living our lives according to our choices.

On Moral Codes

January 19, 1992

Is there something wrong with getting sick? Is there something wrong with getting angry? Is there something wrong with doing anything that violates a moral code? There's nothing wrong with those things. If it attracts you to please God and not do those things, wonderful.

But I don't see how someone could follow the moral code happily by starting off with the idea that they *shouldn't* do those things. All the moral codes of theologies that are based on telling you that you shouldn't do something: there would be no reason to tell you that you shouldn't do something if they didn't believe you wanted to—and if *you* didn't believe you wanted to do what you "shouldn't" do.

When you put yourself in the position of "I want to do these things but I shouldn't," that is unhappiness.

Would happy people violate a moral code? The terrible thing about the question is to imply there are universal rules, instead of phenomena. A happy person is a free person.

Take the commandment not to kill. Could a happy person believe that what you thought was an innocent person, is an enemy? Could any person believe that? Would a happy person protect their own life from an enemy?

When you find yourself in an actual situation, you'll find out the answer. And what do you care until then? When you are in that position, you'll do what *you* want. And if you don't want to kill, you won't, and you won't need any moral code to tell you to do what you want to do.

Any possibility might occur to you: "I could kill, I could not kill." If you're a frightened, scared person, you'll conclude that the possibility must have occurred to you for a reason, and you'll pull the trigger—instead of knowing that it is true: you *could* kill, you could *not* kill—and what do you *want* to do?

COMMENTARIES

by Aryeh Nielsen on

"An Overview of The Option Method"

Choice

This commentary is a synopsis of ideas that Bruce Di Marsico expressed in many writings or talks, but did not express summarily in a single writing or talk.

People don't choose to be unhappy; people don't choose to be happy. I use "choose" only to say something else: unhappiness doesn't happen to you. You're creating it. You're doing it.

I'm using the word choice in a way it was never used before. I'm using it because I'm at a loss for words, because I don't really want to say people want to be unhappy, because they universally describe unhappiness as a feeling they don't want.

BRUCE DI MARSICO

THE use of the word "choice" in Option has been sometimes misconstrued as a statement of direct, active capability to choose beliefs, or to choose happiness. Insofar as someone *does* have the capability to choose beliefs or to choose happiness, they have no use for the Option Method, because they can just be happy.

In Option, unhappiness is a choice *from the point of view of the outside observer*, not from the point of view of the unhappy person. When The Option Method helps someone realize that they do indeed have a choice, that is perfectly simultaneous with no more unhappiness! So from the point of view of the unhappy person, unhappiness is a choice only *retrospectively.*

In fact, Bruce Di Marsico spoke of the danger of the idea of "happiness is a choice" as a seed for being unhappy about being unhappy, because, after all, someone may ask themselves, if it is a choice, why am I choosing to be unhappy?

The Option Method is to help people *find out* that there is a choice with regards to a specific unhappiness. Choice, in Bruce's language, is knowledge of one's inherent freedom, not an action.

A Critique of Therapies

This commentary is a synopsis of ideas that Bruce Di Marsico expressed in many writings or talks, but did not express summarily in a single writing or talk.

Each form of therapy or religion has its own rationale; few exist to help people to be happy. Although many seek help because they are unhappy, what is often offered is an ideal way of living, a standard, a norm.

This is different than helping a person simply to be less unhappy, and to be more happy, and to let them make their own decisions about their life.

I'm not disparaging intentions, here. They have an ideal of what they think a human being could be, and they're trying to see if they can help a person somehow emerge to this newer, better life. But it is the therapy's or religion's idea of a newer and better life.

BRUCE DI MARSICO
NOVEMBER 11, 1995 LECTURE

BRUCE Di Marsico spoke occasionally of Freudian and Reichian therapy, New Age and Existential ideology, and conventional religions. Here, we will look at his critiques, and then summarize the critique in general form.

A Critique of Freudian Therapy

The Option critique of Freudian therapy is quite straightforward.

First, Freudian therapy presumes that past incidents (in particular, childhood incidents) are the cause of present time unhappiness. The Option response is: it is completely irrelevant when a pattern of unhappiness started historically (yesterday, in childhood, or in past lives), because you are believing it is wrong to be as you are right now.

Second, Freudian therapy proposes that perfect happiness is not possible, just being "ordinarily" unhappy. The Option response is: unhappiness is only believed to be necessary; perfect happiness is already your situation, and can never be otherwise, you can only believe that you are unhappy.

Third, Freudian therapy proposes an ideal way of being, the person who is "well-adjusted" to society. The Option response is: happiness is perfectly personal.

A Critique of Reichian therapy

Di Marsico was more sympathetic to Reich than to Freud. The Option critique of Reichian therapy is more nuanced than that of Freudian therapy, and actually points toward how Reichian can (though rarely does) function to help people not need help to be happier.

A Summary of Reichian Therapy

Reichian Therapy conceives of the self in three "layers":

1. The biological core, the natural biological expression of bodily desires
2. The intermediate layer, which is the feeling that natural biological expression of desires would somehow be wrong or bad. This layer is bodily visible as distortions in the expression of biological impulses.
3. The surface layer, which is the social presentation of self, often intended to disguise the intermediate layer.

For example, the desire to be forceful in the biological core, when feared, becomes anger. A social presentation of "being nice" may disguise this anger in social interactions.

Reich and Di Marsico's Terminology

Reichian and Di Marsican terminology are analogous:

REICH	DI MARSICO
The Biological Core	Happy Desiring
The Intermediate Layer	Unhappy Beliefs
The Surface Layer	Acting

By "the biological core," Reich is referring to the bodily expression of happy desiring.

By "the intermediate layer," Reich is referring to the bodily expression of the belief that "to feel as I feel about things would be wrong or bad."

By "the surface layer," Reich is referring to how people may (knowingly) express other than they feel, what Di Marsico called "Acting."

The intermediate and surface layer together are called "armoring," or the bodily expression of unhappiness (the belief that it would be wrong or bad to feel as you do about what happens).

Di Marsico's Criticism of Reich

Bruce Di Marsico criticized some schools of Reichian therapy, saying "Reichian de-armoring is temporary since it does not deal with beliefs."

Here he is criticizing particular schools of Reichian Therapy.

There are two ways Reichian therapy can fail to deal with beliefs.

1. Strategic vs. Relational schools: many schools of Reichian therapy are strategic: they have (to a greater or lesser degree) strategies for treatment. These schools have the medical model: they diagnose and cure. The Option Method is designed only to question an individual's own personal unhappiness, and makes no presumptions whatever about the form of their unhappiness. Very few schools of Reichian therapy are purely relational, meaning they are only interested in what is happening for the client in each moment, and make no diagnostic presumptions.

2. De-armoring (addressing symptoms) vs. cultivating the core (getting in touch with happiness): many schools of Reichian therapy conceive of their task to be breaking down armoring. This is analogous to merely addressing unhappiness. In Option, the purpose of questioning unhappiness is to find the happy motivation behind the unhappiness, and help the person get in touch with that; this yields the revelation that unhappiness is not necessary as motivation, since they are already happily motivated. Again, a few schools of Reichian therapy do focus on cultivating the core, but the vast majority focuses on addressing symptoms.

A Critique of New Age Ideology

The Option critique of New Age ideology is simple: it proposes that you must know or believe something, some esoteric knowledge, in order to be happy. Option proposes that knowledge and beliefs can be the cause of unhappiness, but not happiness, as happiness is just you feeling as you feel, which requires no knowledge or beliefs.

A Critique of Existential Ideology

Existential ideology proposes that unhappiness is necessary (the universe is absurd, etc.). Every bit of Option rejects that proposition.

A Critique of Conventional Religions

Historically, most cultures have agreed that the fundamental "problem" of human existence is not getting what you want.

There have been two main "solutions" (or "cures") for this "problem":

First, to get what you want.

Second, to not want what you want (more elaborately, to achieve a state where you no longer want what you presently want, so that you are no longer at risk of becoming unhappy by means of your desires not being fulfilled).

Self-help philosophies offer ways to get what you want in this life.

Many religions (traditionally known as "Western" religions) propose that you will get everything you want in the afterlife.

Other religions (traditionally known as "Eastern" religions) propose that you are not likely to get everything you want. They propose not wanting as the solution. This is the impossible solution of not wanting to want what you do want. It is true that where there is no wanting, there can be no unhappiness, but someone can only stop wanting what they want if they no longer want it; they cannot "make" themselves stop wanting what they want.

Option offers and describes happiness prior to the question of getting what you want. It proposes that there is no problem with not getting what you want; we need not be unhappy that we don't get what we want. Option also proposes that there is no need to not want what you do want. If we are not unhappy with not having what we want, we do not need to not want what we do want. Stated positively: we can be happy, and want what we want, whether we get it or not.

A Summary of Di Marsico's Critique

Below is a summary of Di Marsico's critique of therapies, comparing the Option point of view to the general therapeutic point of view.

1. You can be happy without getting what you want vs. needing to get what you want, or trying to not want what you want.
2. Perfect happiness is already the case vs. coping with, or adjustment to, unhappiness.
3. Addressing what is happening for the client *now* vs. presuming a cause for feelings outside the client.
4. Happiness is completely personal vs. proposing an ideal way of being.
5. Completely personal course of therapy vs. "diagnosis and cure."
6. Getting in touch with happiness vs. addressing symptoms.
7. No knowledge is necessary for happiness vs. learning knowledge or beliefs.

The Option Attitude, Method, and Teachings

This commentary is based on the editor's understanding of Bruce Di Marsico's teachings.

THE Option Attitude is the tacit, whole-body knowing of happiness. Since this is the inherent attitude of everyone and everything, nothing needs to be done to attain it.

Some, though, mistakenly believe that unhappiness exists (and that it is necessary). Though all desire happiness, as happiness means what each desires most, some fear that happiness is exactly what it is *not*: unhappiness. The experience of unhappiness is the experience of believing that you could value other than what you value, but since you can only value what you value, the experience of unhappiness is the experience of something that does not exist.

For those who mistakenly believe that unhappiness exists (and that it is necessary), The Option Method is a tool for questioning unhappiness, so that its non-necessity (and ultimately, its non-existence) can be recognized. The Option Method is designed to engage presumptions of unhappiness as little as possible, by asking only simple questions that, in themselves, imply nothing.

Though nothing needs to be learned to attain that which is already inherent *as* you (your happiness), there can be much to unlearn to fully recognize your own happiness: the myriad forms of believing that unhappiness exists.

Option teachings are a body of knowledge demonstrating how each form of unhappiness is illusory.

Here is how the Option Attitude, Method, and teachings relate: if you *know* your happiness (the Option Attitude) you do not need to get in touch with your always-already present happiness via The Option Method (which casts away the illusion of unhappiness). Option teachings can aid in a deeper recognition of one's own happiness for those who have become fundamentally *aware* of it.

Myths of Universal Desire

This commentary represents the editor's synthesis of ideas Bruce Di Marsico expressed only in fragments.

HAPPINESS is personal. Your desires are unique to you, even if they appear to be similar to others'. There are many common terms people use which represent an elevation of personal taste to presumptions that all would desire as they desire.

"Healthy" is a paradigm case: being healthy means to have the physical capabilities that *you* desire.

Both the mass media, conventional medicine, and alternative medicine casually use the word "healthy" as if it were a well-defined common standard, like the length of a mile.

"I want to be healthy" is a meaningful statement; it means that you want to have the physical capabilities *you* want. If you ask two people what they mean by "healthy," each will tell you about their personal criteria for judging their physical state.

"He is not healthy" is usually a meaningless statement; if it means "he does not have the physical capabilities I think he should," then it is a proposition that God, nature, or universe somehow define what physical capabilities someone must necessarily have. Since they do not have these capabilities, it is plain to see that these capabilities are not necessary as a "law" of nature or the universe. If "he is not healthy" means "*his* physical capabilities are not what I desire to have as *my* physical capabilities," then the statement is on the order of "he likes pizza, while I like tofu." It is a bringing to awareness of differences in personal preferences.

The paradigm of "healthy" also applies to smart, wealthy, powerful, and many other terms.

Being smart means to have the mental capabilities that *you* desire.

Being wealthy means to have the financial capabilities or property that *you* desire.

Being powerful means to have the social capabilities that *you* desire.

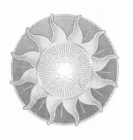

PART II

Happiness

SECTION I

What Is Happiness?

Defining Happiness

THE most summary description of happiness:

> Happiness is the feeling of freedom to the nth degree.
> FROM NOVEMBER 11, 1995 TALK

An elaboration of the above, clarifying that the "freedom" described is perfect freedom of feeling:

> Happiness is feeling however you choose to feel or experience yourself, and not believing that anything makes that wrong.
> FROM WRITING: "YOU CAN BE HAPPY"

Since these feelings are exactly what you most want:

> Happiness is the ultimate desire.
> FROM WRITING: "HAPPINESS HAS NOT NOR EVER HAS BEEN"

Since these feelings are *your* feelings:

> Happiness is the taste in your own mouth.
> FROM NOVEMBER 11, 1995 TALK

Since happiness is perfect knowing of your freedom, as a corollary:

> Unhappiness is the belief that you're not free.
> FROM DECEMBER 5, 1987 TALK

Specifically, unhappiness is believing you are not free to feel the way you like:

Unhappiness is believing we have to forbid ourselves the feelings we like.

FROM WRITING: "THE TWO PRINCIPLES"

And to forbid ourselves the feelings we like can be described as being against ourselves:

Unhappiness is believing that you are against yourself.

FROM WRITING: "ONE TRUTH"

Our experience of not feeling free to feel as we would like (right now) is only and entirely our experience of the belief that at some point we may have to forbid ourselves the feelings we like.

Unhappiness is the belief that unhappiness can and will happen in the future.

FROM DECEMBER 5, 1987 TALK

Since we never have to forbid ourselves the feelings we like:

Unhappiness doesn't exist. It isn't real. It seems to exist as a result of a simple belief and the subsequent beliefs that naturally follow from that belief.

FROM WRITING: "UNHAPPINESS DOESN'T EXIST"

About Happiness
November 11, 1995

In the talk "About Happiness," Bruce Di Marsico introduces and discusses more about what happiness is and how unhappiness happens.

He describes the feeling of happiness as a feeling of perfect freedom, which is our inherent state, and how there is never a problem with feeling happy.

He talks about how we feel "right now" as we predict we will feel in the future.

He addresses the myth that another person's unhappiness could be contagious. He also distinguishes between unhappiness, and happily valuing something negatively; for example, happily deciding that you don't want to see a particular movie.

THE point I'm trying to make is that The Option Method is to help people to not need help. Do you understand that's essential? Because people believe they need help to not be unhappy.

Heretofore on this planet one has believed that the only way to stop being unhappy was to have power over those things that make us unhappy; that the only way to not be unhappy was to have power over those things that are the cause of our unhappiness or may be the cause of our unhappiness. That's what we sought. Love to cure all the unhappinesses of not being loved. Health to cure all the unhappinesses of illness and disease and pain. Wealth to cure all the unhappinesses of not being able to have the things you want. And they were the answers, the only answers we could have.

So people would try to have any of those three things and they'd always usually be the center of people's fears and unhappiness.

I haven't used the word fear, but I'm going to. Unhappinesses work in a certain way. They work because they're in the future. The only cause of unhappiness is believing you're going to be unhappy. [Believing] that in the future you'll be unhappy. Only a belief in the future can make you unhappy.

I love my dirty little tricks and one is this: If you knew at this time tomorrow that you'd be really unhappy what would you be now?

If you believed you were going to be unhappy tomorrow, you'd be unhappy now. You can't believe you're going to be unhappy tomorrow and wait. You just can't. You're going to be unhappy now. That's the way it works. Even though the unhappiness is now, the belief is about the future.

If you believe that this time tomorrow you are going to be radiantly happy, how would you feel now? Radiantly happy. It doesn't even have to happen for us to feel it. The thing is in our believing and our feeling. The dynamics, the cause of our emotions, is in our beliefs about tomorrow. There never has to be a tomorrow. That's why you can be happy forever, because today you can be happy forever.

It's your knowing that you're going to be happy forever which can make you extraordinarily happy right now. Your knowing you're going to be happy for the rest of your life would make you happy from this moment on, wouldn't it? So that's all you're missing. All you need is to know you're going to be happy for the rest of your life. That's all.

Okay. Well, maybe we can do something about that. The Option Method comes in there because what you're suffering from is believing that there'll be some limit to your happiness and that you will be unhappy from time to time and that you won't be happy for the rest of your life.

Or perhaps you fully expected to be happy now, forever, and for the rest of your life. Well, you can be, but you can't be happy if you are always looking to see if happiness is still there or if it has disappeared.

Happiness is something that happens to you in the same way unhappiness did. It has to be felt as happening to you or it won't feel like happiness. It won't feel sincere. It won't feel real and I have no quarrel with how we feel happiness. That's not a problem.

Happiness generally is going to have to feel like it happens to you. You're not going to be able to crank it up because it works by the same mechanisms. The same dynamics, as I like to say. Since we don't have machinery parts in us I like to talk about dynamics, which means thoughts working against other thoughts with other thoughts and in conjunction with other thoughts, as opposed to other thoughts, in addition to other thoughts. Those are called dynamics.

All the various thoughts sorting themselves out are the dynamics of a human being and all the various motions within the body are the symptoms of those dynamics.

Happiness is of course a symptom of a certain dynamic that takes place within the body. People will like to talk to you about certain hormones that cause that feeling of happiness, but actually it only simulates it and it's similar to it. It's not the same. The feeling of happiness is a feeling of freedom to the nth degree, extreme freedom. That's not the feeling of being high. That simulates it and appears like it.

A person who's really happy really knows that they're really free. I'm using the word "really" in order to underline it. That's all. You can forget the underlines. A person who's happy knows that they're free. That is what we call the most wonderful, beautiful feeling in the world. So nobody can define happiness for you. That's stupid. I would never define happiness for *you*. For all I know it tastes horrible to *me*.

Happiness is the taste in your own mouth. Remember that. No one else can know that sweetness, that joy because it's your freedom. The only happiness you can ever relate to, the only happiness you can ever know, except perhaps for God's if there is a God who can do this, is your own happiness. That's the only happiness you can know.

If you knew another person's happiness you'd be happy and you'd be knowing your happiness. So happiness is yours and it's like the taste in your own mouth. No one else can judge it and no one else can experience it. Now we can see symptoms of it and be glad for that. "Hey, you look like you're in a good mood today, Charlie." Something like that.

But nonetheless the real happiness is in the person. Well, the same is true about unhappiness, regardless of what you hear, unhappiness is the taste in the unhappy person's mouth. Although you can sympathize and although you can reproduce those feelings in yourself, you can be sensitive, you can be hypersensitive, but that's like anything else.

You're willing to feel that way, but if you're a psychic actually you only feel it physically. You don't need to feel it as a judgment you made if you didn't make that judgment.

Let's say you walk in a room with a whole bunch of depressed people and all of a sudden you sense that there is depression in the room. You have no intention of being depressed, but somehow you sense it physically. Well, as long as you can tell the difference between what you're sensing and what you're creating, no problem.

Well, since you wouldn't have a reason to create the feeling, you would know you were sensing it. If you don't have a reason to create the feeling, well then you might be like half the hypochondriacs in the world. They don't like the vibes in this room. So, that's just agoraphobia. That's just another form of unhappiness and fear.

They're sensing it and believing and are afraid that it'll affect them. The only reason I'd be afraid of unhappiness is if I thought it could reach out to me and grab my heart, but if I don't have any such belief that any unhappiness in a person could do that, I could never fear another person's unhappiness, right? That's how we can practice The Option Method by the way.

I've seen the most extreme unhappinesses that you can imagine on this planet and my desire was to help them; not to root it out of myself somehow.

Compassion and sympathy are two different things. Compassion is wanting to help a person know, who wants to know, that maybe they don't have to be unhappy since what I know is that their unhappiness is based on some beliefs of theirs. But the way I would put it to a person who believes that they have to be unhappy in the first place, compassion would be helping somebody who feels that they have no choice about being unhappy to see how the dynamics work. How they brought it into being by their beliefs.

Now for people to say, or for any of us to say we don't intend to be unhappy anytime we're unhappy, that's just simply not true. If we look close enough you'll see there's something good about it. There's something that we hope it'll do. Something acceptable in it or we wouldn't be having it.

We're not just merely terrified of it and if we are just merely terrified of it that's because we believe that being terrified of it has got some salvific grace—that there's something healing about being terrified about unhappiness.

So there are people who hate unhappiness. That's not new. Or they're hating sin or anything else. They think by doing such a thing that they're somehow creating a more healthy salvific atmosphere. That's all. That's just a belief. That's all. They're not doing that. They're just experiencing fear and hatred.

The other part of unhappiness is fear, and fear and unhappiness are the same. Fear is being afraid of being unhappy.

Unhappiness is being afraid that you're going to be happy when you shouldn't be. I didn't tell you that before. I just snuck it in. But that's what we found out through the third question. "Why are you afraid not to be unhappy?"

We find that out in the long run, bottom line, although we don't really explain this to ourselves when we get unhappy, see, because remember unhappiness makes you stupid. So we're not so smart as to explain this to ourselves or we wouldn't do it. Unhappiness happens in the dark. It happens in the half light of reason. It happens somewhere in that period when you're waking up in the morning and you wake up. It's not something you can see clearly or you wouldn't do it. "Oh yes, I think I'll drive a nail through my head." No, I don't think so.

It happens in the half light. And so the reasoning is not very good because unhappiness makes us stupid. We are afraid to be happy. What we're afraid of is that if we were happy we'd be a way we shouldn't be.

So I said fear was the fear of becoming unhappy, but unhappiness is the fear of not being unhappy. Understand me? Even if you don't understand how it goes I'll try to explain it, but you know the words so far.

Start with this. First of all, no one is afraid of poverty. People are afraid of being poor and unhappy. No one is afraid of pain. People are afraid of pain and the unhappiness that comes with it. Nobody's afraid of loss, but the loss and unhappiness. Nobody's afraid of death, but the death and the unhappiness that comes with it. Nobody's afraid of dying, but the unhappiness that comes with it.

There is no thing that any human being is afraid of. So it is very easy to do The Option Method. We ask people what they're afraid of and it doesn't matter what they say because they're not afraid of that.

None of you are afraid and have ever been afraid of anything you said you were afraid of. Did you know that? You never were afraid of anything you said you were afraid of. All you were afraid of was the unhappiness that you thought went with it. That's the rationale of The Option Method.

And why wouldn't you be? So whatever you thought would bring unhappiness with it you'd be afraid of. Even love can be frightening. We put people down. It's fashionable to do so.

Say people are afraid of commitment as if that was some kind of a bad thing, but they're not afraid of the commitment part. They're afraid of the bad part. They're afraid of whatever that is in there that'll make them unhappy, which is probably breaking the commitment or being turned off to the commitment. All commitments are made as a person honestly estimating themselves.

It seems to them that they could love you forever when they say that, just before sunrise or something, or just before that moment that Meatloaf talks about.

We believe ourselves. We don't necessarily mean to lie. We really do believe that we're going to love this forever and love that forever and be here forever and do that for as long as we live. We're talking about present conditions staying the same, forever.

It doesn't take into account that that they've turned into a horrible person, even though they say "Oh, you'll never be a horrible person in my eyes." Those are people who just don't understand you. Well, those are wonderful things to hear and fools mean them sometimes, but they're not lying and they're not afraid of commitment in that sense.

What they're afraid of is that what they're promising isn't what you think they're promising and they're afraid that you think they're promising something other than what they're saying. What they're saying is "I, as I know myself, as I believe myself to be, will do this and will do that. I'll see you Saturday in front of the movie theater at eight o'clock." I honestly thought I would do that and if I don't show up Saturday at eight o'clock it isn't because I'm afraid of commitment. It's because of whatever it's because of.

Now, if it's because of between now and Saturday, I start thinking of you, and every time I think of going to the theater with you, I start thinking "What am I going to do after the theater with you? Oh no!" Then I think it again.

"Okay, I'm going to meet her at the theater," and then I think about *after* the theater and—"No, no." Every time I come up with a "no, no" I come closer and closer to not coming at eight o'clock. I wasn't a liar. I was just headstrong.

Maybe I wasn't fully honest about what it would all entail. Maybe

I just didn't think things through. So all I'm saying is that people are accused of things that are actually very nice things and then they're being accused of being afraid of those things, which they really aren't afraid of. They're only afraid of them under another name.

Nobody's afraid of commitment to something that they love. So, you know what I'm saying? So the word fear can't be used that way.

What I'm trying to say is that unhappiness is the fear of happiness. Fear is the fear of unhappiness. In other words, you were never afraid of any of the things you've ever thought you were afraid of. All you were afraid of was the unhappiness that you thought would go with them. That's just simply a truth.

There are no exceptions to it. I've never heard an exception. There are no possibilities of exceptions. Feel free if you come up with any.

And happiness is just that. Being happy. We all know what happy means and it's feeling really free. There is no question of your being wrong, period. There's just no question that the way you feel is the best way to feel. No question. And the point of "no question" is very important, because The Option Method is questions.

So happiness is when unhappiness is no longer a question and you don't need The Option Method to know that you don't have to question your happiness because there's no unhappiness to question.

You would never question your happiness, right? If you're happy you don't question your happiness. So it's something we don't discuss in the early stages of the practice of The Option Method at all because first of all we unhappy people are not really competent to discuss happiness and its causes and lack of causes and where it leads to and what it'll do. No, no, no. That's not the point. You'll be happy. You know how to be happy. And you will know how to be happy.

That's not the problem. The problem is, you're thinking that you know you have to be unhappy. The fear of unhappiness causes unhappiness. That can be easily understood pretty quickly in our lives.

So that every time you're unhappy it's because you're fearing unhappiness. That's all. Even if you're fearing that you're stupid and you didn't learn The Option Method correctly. That can keep you unhappy for the rest of your life.

Anything that you say, anything that you can identify where you believe it's natural for you to have to be unhappy, I suggest that it's questionable. That it can be questioned. I suggest, and I say to you, "But what if what you're feeling is just really a result of a belief you have or a judgment you're making?

"Would you like to examine it for the possibility that maybe you could feel better?" And that's what The Option Method practitioner offers. Would you like to examine what you call your unhappiness to see if you could be happier? That's all.

So in The Option Method what I want to know is if a person is asking for help with their unhappiness or they're asking for advice. Sometimes people hear that there's a wise person around and they want to know whether they need therapy or not, whether they're normal or not or whether they should leave their husband or not or whether they should quit their job or not.

They've heard that there's a wise person around and they want to use them and pick their brains or they've learned that they've decided that they were too negative and they want to be positive. Whatever that means. That makes me dizzy that somehow being positive is better than being negative. I don't think so.

I think that there are things that we love feeling positive about and there are things that we love that we feel negative about and that doesn't have anything to do with unhappiness.

You probably have very few positive feelings about being run over by a bus. I doubt it. Unless you value yourself as fertilizer. If you promised your parents fertilizer, I can see your point.

But there are lots of things that you simply value negatively. That's not a problem. But people come to what they think a wise person is looking for all kinds of possibilities, and all I'm interested in is their unhappiness. That's my only field of competence.

People in The Option Method do not interpret dreams, do not lend you rent money, do not give you advice about your guru, do not try to substitute for your sacraments at church, don't try to take the place of your parents. I don't even like to give geographical directions because I'm not all that good at it.

But giving advice is not our field. That's all. It's just not our field and we just want to keep it straight that why you're here is, if you're a client of mine, is because you want help with your unhappiness. You want help to be less unhappy.

No Thing Gives Happiness
June 1982

No thing in the world gives happiness. No thing or lack of any thing causes unhappiness. Happiness is.

Unhappiness is believing, in practice, that we need help to be happy or we need something (help) to avoid that need or the condition of need.

Unhappiness is the fear of not believing we have needs in case we are wrong and really do need help to not be unhappy. It is believing that we may really have needs that need to satisfied even though we don't like being that way (i.e., needy).

It doesn't matter if we don't get what we have learned or believed is "good." Our meaning of "good" is "that which satisfies or prevents a need." No thing prevents need. No thing causes need. We have just merely believed in need.

Your Unhappiness Is Caused by a Belief

YOUR unhappiness is caused by a belief of yours.
What belief?

The belief that you could be unhappy for some cause other than a certain belief of yours.

Which certain belief is that?

None. You don't have the belief necessary to cause unhappiness except for the above belief that it could exist from a cause other than this certain belief that you would have to have, but which you don't.

What would that belief have to be to create unhappiness?

The belief that unhappiness could never exist no matter what you believed.

In a most real sense, this is your contribution to the universe and to your happiness. You have the power to keep unhappiness out.

By believing that it is not caused by you or your beliefs, you are proving in the only way possible that you are the cause of its existence and the cause of its non-existence.

That belief is the cause of apparent unhappiness.

Knowing that only your belief can cause unhappiness would only make you unhappy if you knew you had such a belief that could cause it, other than the above belief.

The only belief that could cause it would be a true denial of your power to believe.

"Unhappiness could never exist even if I believed that it could exist apart from my beliefs." I.e., "My beliefs are impotent. My believing does not have the nature of believing but is empty thought that I am not thinking, but only think I think."

Degrees of Happiness

Happiness is the ground for giving ourselves the feelings we like and want.

Unhappiness is the ground for believing we have to forbid ourselves the feelings we like. We therefore experience feelings we dislike as if we were the unwitting victim of such bad feelings.

"Degrees of happiness" is the experience of allowing our bodies to respond to our awareness now in direct proportion to implications of getting more of what we want in the future.

We are glad for:

1. Getting what we usually get.
2. Getting what we hope to get, but don't usually.
3. Getting more than we even hoped for.
4. Getting more than that.

We are glad (happier by degrees or intensity) according to our awareness (belief) that what we are getting is to whatever degree allowing or productive of getting more of what we want more or want most:

e.g., glad for money,
more glad for health,
more glad for love,
most glad for God.

The basic belief of all mankind is that the happier we are for getting what we want (especially more than we hoped for), the more our happiness will be dependent on it, and our happiness will therefore become unhappiness if the "more than what we hoped for" is taken away from us or if we destroy it. So they begin to become afraid of getting more than what they want, and lose attraction and desire for it. Their feelings die. They now only want "the simple things," the ordinary thing, the reliable and substitutable things, average things. "Don't tempt me with more than I hoped for, it scares me. I haven't yet learned to cope with losing ordinary things like money, friends, sex, fun, etc. These things at least can always be hoped for in other versions if they go away and happiness can return."

But there is no other "what perfectly suits me." There is no other "perfectly all that I could ever want or hope for."

SECTION II

Facets of Happiness

Perfect Self-Trust

March 17, 1976

In this writing, Bruce Di Marsico discusses perfect self-trust.

Perfect self-trust is knowing our desires are the best for ourselves. Bruce Di Marsico shows that our desires can only be what is best for ourselves; if we are believing that our desires are not best for ourselves, that can only be because we are aware of desires that are better for ourselves, which are also our desires, and what we want more. Therefore, it is impossible to be mistaken about what is best for us.

Accepting someone's advice is when our knowing what's best for us coincides with what someone thinks is best for us. If two people coincide in point of view, they do not have the "same" point of view. Rather, in a moment, for all practical purposes, two individuals' point of view is relatively coincident. Our point of view is always ours, and never someone else's.

When we are trusting ourselves, our decisions on behalf of others will be as good for them as their own self-trusting decisions.

WE believe that we should be feeling good and being happy regardless of what we think and do. We believe that first we should feel good for no reason and then think and do what we would love to think and do.

Isn't the truth better?

Being happy and feeling good comes from the "way" we think. The "way" we think means how we think of what we think. If we judge our thoughts and desires as not the best way to think and want, we have believed that the "best" way (meaning, what is most productive and useful for *me*) is not our way—this is the equivalent of believing that I am not the best me for me to start with. I need another me. I need to be changed, a miracle, a transformation, a death and resurrection. I need a new me.

What we feel and feel like doing come from what we believe (think). This is truth. There is no other way. If we think (believe) there may be another truth then we will feel accordingly. We will *feel* dissatisfied with the above statement. See! What we think produces the appropriate feeling.

The only truth regarding happiness—true, real, felt happiness—is this: you are the best for you. Your decisions are the best. Your desires are the best. What you think is the best way of thinking for you. You, as you are, are the best you for others. There is nothing about you that is not the best for you getting what you want. You are the best you for having what you want. What you forget is best forgotten. When you remember, it is the best time for you to remember. What you like to eat, when you want to sleep, what you love to have, who you want to have love you, etc., is the best thing for you. When or if you change your mind, then that will be the best time to change your mind and that is the best change for you.

You know what is best for you. You absolutely know it. You cannot be wrong. It is impossible that you can be mistaken.

If another suggests something to you about what to think or what to want or how to do, because you know what is best for you, you will know, absolutely know, whether they are right or not. You know when you recognize what you want in their suggestion.

If they are right about what you want, if you now realize something you hadn't realized, it is not because you do not know what is best for you, it is precisely because you do know that what you want is best for you.

If you didn't become aware until another made you aware it is because you know it was the best time to be aware. If another tells you a truth that you recognize and you realize that you have not been aware before, that is because you know what is best for you. If it were better for you to have known sooner you would have made yourself aware sooner.

You are the best way of being yourself and being happy.

It only seems like we weren't because we believed otherwise.

Isn't it perfect that if we believe that we are bad for ourselves, we should feel bad, unsure, untrusting, crazy?

We believed that *if* we were good for ourselves we would always be happy and sure and confident and doing what pleased us.

No. That is wrong. Impossible. If that were true we would be lost. We would be truly hopeless, not only feeling hopeless. It is enough that that attitude makes us feel hopeless. If it were true we would also know we were hopeless and instantly die.

Because we begin with "if" we are still indicating our belief that we may not be best for ourselves. Change "if" to "since": Since I am best for me and you are best for you . . . If I believe you are also best for me that is because since I am best for me I can decide that you are too. I cannot be wrong. It cannot be that I believe you are best for me because I believe I am not best for me, but only because I am. If I were to believe that you are best because I am not, then I will doubt even that decision and not really believe you are best for me. You are not best for me because only you believe you are best for me or because you are best for me by some outside magic, but because, since I am best for me, I can think or know that you are also all I want for me. It is not because I lack anything for my fullness that I love you, but simply because I am sure of my desires and decisions as best for me. When you are sure of you, your decisions for me are as good as mine. When I am sure of me, my decisions are as good for you as yours.

I cannot be bad for you any more that I can be bad for myself.

What I think about me makes all the difference. Shouldn't it?

Should I feel honest when I think I may not be?

Should I feel happy when I think I may not be?

Should I feel happy when I think that I ought to be happy before I deserve to enjoy myself?

If I believe that doing or thinking what I would most love to think or do must wait until I'm happy, how will I become happy?

Happiness does not come from that kind of thinking or from doing that kind of thinking.

Happiness comes from thinking and acting, happily. Not acting *like* a happy person or trying to think *like* a happy person, but from being happy and believing and behaving happily.

It means be happy about how you think and what you want. Be happy to do what you want and do it the way you would most love to.

Let yourself happen. You're best. The way you'll happen is happy and beautiful and true.

Happiness is! Happiness lives in you. It directs every beat of your heart, every thought, every desire, every movement in your body. Everything. Absolutely everything.

Perfection is moving you. You are now perfect.

Happiness Is Feeling
However You Choose

January 6, 1991

Happiness is feeling however you choose to feel or experience yourself, and not believing that anything makes that wrong.

Happiness is knowing (or not denying) that nothing can make you feel other than how you really do feel, and nothing will make you feel other than you really do feel.

Unhappiness is believing that you are against yourself.

Unhappiness is believing that something *means* you are against yourself.

Unhappiness is believing that something you want or don't want means you are against yourself.

Unhappiness is believing that something you want or don't want means you are against yourself and your future happiness.

Unhappiness is believing that something you think or don't think means you are against yourself and your future happiness.

Unhappiness is believing that something you do or don't do means you are against yourself and your future happiness.

Unhappiness is believing that *you* are not the way you should be.

Unhappiness is believing that being happy *now* is not being the way you should be.

SECTION III

Motivation

Motivation Is the Cause of Movement

MOTIVATION is that which causes movement.

A baby who begins to walk does not walk because they want to walk; a baby wants to get somewhere. The baby fixes his attention on a goal, on a place, and wants to go there. That's the wanting that's involved. If he's happy, he will walk if he's able. If he's unable to walk he may crawl if he's able. In other words he wants to get somewhere the easiest, or perhaps the most efficient way he can. So he's not aware of deciding, "I think I will walk." That's a very sophisticated concept we have no reason to believe that a baby is at all interested in.

You pretty much motivate yourself the same way. If you're sitting where you're sitting and you want to go to the toilet, I don't even know whether you toss it over in your mind whether you'll crawl in or hop in. Maybe you just let yourself know that you want to be in there and then everything takes over from that. Just by wanting it and wanting to be there the easiest way perhaps, or the most efficient way perhaps. You'll just walk to be there, you'll do whatever is in your power to get there.

Very frequently we think that achieving things lies in wanting the intermediate steps. There are going to be very few of us who are going to want to walk for no reason at all, who are just going to want to walk for the sake of walking, which brings us into the whole concept of wanting as a motivation. The wanting of something is really the wanting of something else. Behind every want is a want for something else: I want this for that other thing that I want, and I want that for something else that I want (I'm using the word wanting and desiring synonymously.)

Happiness Is Our Ultimate Desire

Aᴌᴌ desires are to serve other desires, and ultimately the chain ends at something we call happiness. Just like the series of fears that we investigate through The Option Method (we're unhappy that we fear *this* because we fear *that* because we fear . . .)—so things that are desired are connected the same way.

In The Option Method investigation, we investigate, "Why are you unhappy about this?" "Well, because I fear *that*." "Why are you unhappy about that?" "Because I fear *this*." Just as that chain leads to an underlying belief so does exploring the reasons for desire. Nothing is wanted in and of itself, or for itself. Everything is wanted for another thing that's wanted. This very process of wanting for something else that we want is called rationality.

So motivation is the cause of movement. Desiring, wanting a goal, brings the intermediate steps into play because they're wanted for the goal. The baby doesn't want the walking, he wants to be somewhere, therefore he brings the walking into play. It can be said, and as he gets older he may even articulate it as wanting to walk, but that isn't what he really wants. He wants to be somewhere.

No child will be able to walk unless he's physically able to walk, and nor will he walk unless he has a reason to, a goal. And be very clear that a child who lives in a small area will not walk as quickly or as easily as a child who lives in a larger area. A child who can crawl to everything that he crawls to, as long as that is physically easier to do will do so. When the child wants something and wants to get it more easily, more efficiently, and the legs are able to do it, it'll happen.

We wouldn't think that crawling is an easier thing to do right now, but yet somehow it's easier for a baby. We don't even need to know or make the decision, the body does.

So desire is motivation insofar as it's the cause of movement. And all desire is the desire for something else, and all desires for something else are the desire for something else beyond that. It's all for something.

More Happy vs. Less Unhappy

You're wanting money, for example, for some reasons, such as "to not work at a job everyday." And you want it in order to be free and you want freedom because you believe that that can make you happy somehow, right?

I guess anywhere along the line we could say it'd make us happy. I want money, so we normally would say, "If I had money it'd make me happy." What do I want it for? "Because I want to be free and I believe freedom will make me happy." All wanting is wanting for something else so I might want money in order to have material things, I want material things in order to take care of my freedom or to take care of my health or to take care of whatever. And I want all of that so that I can do this and do that, and I want that so that I can be happy. But maybe that last jump is magical. Maybe it's really mythical.

Why do we want any of these things in order to be happy? Why do we believe that these things will give us the happiness? But, nonetheless, that becomes what's called rationale or rationality: wanting for a reason. We make up the final reasons as, "It'll make me happy," which is self-defining.

And if you notice that a lot of people are afraid to get in touch with why they want something because they sense that somehow it is magical, that there isn't really anything there. "Why do you want that?" "What do you mean why do I want it?" You get that kind of an answer, especially if the wanting comes from fear.

Now if wanting isn't from fear and we're not using fear to motivate ourselves, but we're just using strictly desire, you will still run into the ultimate point where there's a belief involved. "I believe that after I have all of these things, after I have health and wealth, power or goods and material things, and freedom, I will then be happy."

"If I don't get it, then I'll be unhappy" changes wanting into needing. And that we're all very familiar with. Needing becomes the alternate way of motivating oneself. Needing doesn't have to follow from not getting. Instead, what could follow not getting is "If I don't have it, I don't have it."

And wouldn't it depend on where you're at now? If I don't have it, I'm where I'm at now. All right, where am I now? If I'm unhappy, if I don't have it I'll be unhappy; if I'm happy if I don't have it I'll still be happy. So it depends on where you happen to be at the moment you started wanting.

Happy Motivation

Money and love become two symbols in our culture, which stems from the belief that you can't be happy now, that there's something lacking, something needed. Lacking in the sense: I'd be unhappy without it, but I won't be more happy with it. And unhappy people motivate themselves with the belief that, "I'll be unhappy without it."

Happy people tend to motivate themselves with the belief that I won't be more happy unless I have it. But it's a similar set of rules. It's an easier game to play because—all right, I won't be more happy if I *don't* have that, but I could be more happy if I have that or that.

There are a lot more things that could make a happy person happier. Maybe it's the whole universe, maybe the whole world of things. And maybe, if you had the indomitably happy person and he said, "I can't be more happy unless I have that," and you say, "You can't have it," then he'd say, "Well, then this," and you say, "You can't have it," he might spend the rest of his life saying, "Well, then this." And that'd be okay because he wouldn't lose, he'd be so busy saying, "Well, then this," because there'd always be another "this," and it's not too hard a game to play.

And even when it came down to the end of it, "Okay, well, then the next breath, and that'll make me more happy," with a happy person none of it becomes a bad place to be, ever, even though he's believing or she's believing that they need it to be more happy, but they don't need it for their happiness. And if everything else goes away and you absolutely can't have anything it would seem, you make up something. Like another moment, "If I could have another moment I'll be happier."

And if you say, "You can't have another moment," then the happy person says, "Well, then—" and at that moment their life is over.

Intermediate Steps

So wanting a goal makes the intermediary steps take place. It actually creates them. If you want to go to New York tonight, that wanting to go to New York will make all the intermediary steps take place, whatever those steps are going to be. Fearing that you will remain in New Jersey can also make the intermediary steps take place, at the cost of unhappiness and with the risk of taking self-defeating action. But wanting to go to New York can make all the intermediary steps take place, insofar as they're within our power, insofar as they're within our ability, insofar as they are natural to the human being that we are in the universe. Whether it means taking a bus, asking for a ride, starting our car, making sure the car is in working condition. There are countless numbers of phenomena and factors involved, all of which we've apparently taking care of without much thought. Your gas tanks have gas in it, your cars are in working order, you have spare tires. All of those factors have already been taken into consideration and you didn't even run through a checklist, probably, but you want something to be, you want it to happen and all the intermediary steps will take place for you. You will make sure of them insofar as you can make sure of them.

And there's no reason why they won't unless you're unhappy: if you're unhappy you may have been neglecting your tires. If you're unhappy you may not have filled your gas tank. If you're unhappy you may not have taken care of yourself, you may not have arranged to ask somebody for a ride back and they may be gone before you think of asking them, things like that.

But you would then really not be in touch with your goal. So then it follows that the more a thing is wanted the more possible and the more easy is its eventuality. Wanting is what makes things happen, what makes us move, what changes things in our world, and the more we want, the more possible and the more easy is the eventuality. If we were always in touch with wanting there would be no unhappiness; unhappiness is what we do when we've doubted that we may remember our goal, and it's the way that we remind ourselves.

SECTION IV

Expressions of Happiness

Gratitude

WE are grateful when we are realizing that we are getting something that we had no power to make happen.

I am grateful that my painter does such a nice job because I know that there is no way I could make him do the job he has done so well. He could have done less and I would have accepted that I got what I paid for. When I have the feeling that I got more than I bargained for, it is the awareness that he does his thing for his reasons, but whatever they are, I am still glad I was the recipient. Even if he did extra just to earn my gratitude (which is good business for him) I am glad that he did. I am glad I don't have to be on his back to get what I want. I am glad he makes things easy for me. I am glad that he gives me what I can't be sure I would have if he didn't give it to me.

My feeling of gratitude prompts me to encourage him and reward him somehow so that he knows what he did was appreciated by me. I want him to know that he is appreciated and that my appreciation could be good for him. I thank him a lot. I show concern that he feels he is getting enough money. I offer him references. I hope he will always do any painting I need done.

I want to express my gratitude so that I feel I do not take this for granted, as if it didn't matter, as if I didn't know he did more for me than I hoped for. Even though *I* know I am not unsurprised, unmoved, and ungrateful, I want to express it to him.

I know that he can only want to do a better thing if he knows it really *is* better. I may *think* it is better, but I do not know that *he* knows he has done better for me unless I express it. Then I am sure. If he believes me, then he will know that what he expended special care and effort for really *was* better. My expression of gratitude tells him that it was worth the effort to me too. If he believed me it may then be, or continue to be, worth it to him since he now can know it truly is better.

Whatever prompted him to do better for me, he would not do it if he believed that it was *not* better, or even worse, in my eyes. If it was to make me happy, he would not want to do it if it seemed *not* to make me happy.

If I give what I give so that others can be happier then I will only give it if I see that they truly *are* happier with it. If it becomes a gift to scorn, or be confused or frightened of then I do not want to give it. My purpose in giving peace, for example, is to give peace. If my gift of peace is the occasion of fear and distrust and suspicion and self-hate and jealousy and resentment I do not want to give it. I do not want to give a gift of peace if it does not really give peace. If I think they are really grateful for my gift, but are having trouble or fears expressing it though, then I may still want to give it. If what I give is worth it to others, then they will do what it takes to get it. If not, should it be otherwise?

Doubts, Signs, and Rituals

February 15, 1974

THE heart, in its ever-seeking to manifest its perfection to itself, seeks and makes occasions for affirmation of its goodness and perfection.

When we begin on the path of new life, we want to establish a firm hold on our new beliefs in happiness.

While we are going through the period of fearing that we lack justification and reasons for our selfish, unreasonable yearning for perfect happiness (in the knowledge that we cannot "make" ourselves unhappy) we find that we are confronting the inevitable fact that we are totally good and perfect regardless of the so-called "evidence."

This is the "hardest" and, of course, the only thing we ever faced. While it would seem helpful to us to experience a miracle (that which is awesome without reason) which would "prove" we were blessed and good, it would not really help in that way. If you do not believe what you already know, you would only fear that you grasped at the miracle for proof, as if you didn't know what you knew, and be even more doubtful.

It is not as a sign of our knowing, nor as proof to us of our believing what we already know, that we want miracles. If there are to be useful miracles in our life, it is precisely because we don't need them. It would be a sign, not that we *may* indeed really believe what we already know, but that we *do* indeed really believe what we already know.

If we know (without doubt) that we believe what we already know, then a miracle will be a cause of joy and gladness, a gift precisely because it was unneeded. If we experience a miracle while in doubt, besides doubting the miracle, we will also resent it as an unwanted gift precisely because it was needed. The bigger the miracle, the bigger each response.

If we know we are being blessed, and becoming blessed beings, we will respond. The response is our sign to ourselves that we really believe what we already know. I am doing what I am doing because I am glad to be *aware* that I believe what I know.

If we do not respond with some sign that we recognize as an affirmation of gratitude and joy, we may respond with some sign which will mean to us whatever it is that we fear we believe in, in spite of what we know. Our bodies can show us what we fear we believe, or they will show what we know we believe. Peace or pain. A smile or a frown. Praise or sarcasm. Generosity or envy.

The mind is of the body. The brain will present all kinds of lies to the man who fears he is a liar, and present doubts to the doubter. This is the heart's way of leading itself to perfect happiness. For the person who fears to externalize signs of affirmation, the mind will present opportunities for internal affirmations.

If I fear to dance with joy, my mind will present me with the thoughts that perhaps I am really sad and dour. This is a moment of fantastic, beautiful temptation. It is our natural given opportunity to affirm what we really believe.

"I refuse to believe that I could be sad. I know that I have nothing to be dour about. I really believe that I'm okay."

If we do not respond to these heart urgings in the mind truthfully, that is, happily consistent with the truth we know, then the relentless love in our heart will continually present these doubts until we acquiesce to what we know. To the one who persistently refuses to believe, the thoughts will seem like assaults, the movements in the body will seem like torture. They are not attacks and assaults, but are the prompting questions of love manifesting themselves so that finally we can accept the happiness that we yearn so ardently for.

These so-called symptoms of unhappiness are not evidence of anything, not one thing else other than refusing to believe what we know, namely that we are blessed, happy, godly and perfectly okay.

They could not happen except as a result of a miracle.

Your Self is continually trying to tell you that you are beautiful, happy and have nothing to fear.

COMMENTARIES

by Aryeh Nielsen on

"Happiness"

Happiness Is Not a Mood

This commentary represents the editor's synthesis of ideas Bruce Di Marsico expressed only in fragments.

1. Happiness, from the Option point of view, is the (tacit, whole-body) knowledge that there are no problems with anything. In particular, there is nothing wrong with you, and nothing wrong with others, and nothing wrong with the world. If you know this, you will certainly not be unhappy. Nothing more is necessary.
2. In conventional society, many moods are described as happiness, including:
    a. moods of present-time pleasure, experienced physically in the present, such as cheerfulness and sexual arousal.
    b. moods of present-time satisfaction, experienced physically in the present, such as equanimity ("being centered") and calm.
    c. moods of satisfaction with the remembered (past) self, such as pride in success and contentment in accomplishments.
    d. moods of meaning, experienced when contemplating the (imagined) future self, such as purposefulness and calling.

   Can you be sexually aroused and unhappy? Consider the compulsive masturbator. Can you be calm and unhappy? Consider those who take tranquilizers in order to "deal with" their life. Can you be successful and unhappy? Consider the stories of tabloid magazines. Can you have a meaningful life and be unhappy? For some, the meaning of life is stress, strain, and struggle.

5. Considering these moods which are generally claimed to be related to happiness, from the Option point of view:
   Relative to the present:

   In particular, happiness is the (tacit, whole-body) knowledge that there is nothing wrong with your present-time mood.
    a. There is nothing wrong with you, others, or the universe if you are not cheerful.

b. There is nothing wrong with you, others, or the universe if you are not sexually aroused.

c. There is nothing wrong with you, others, or the universe if you are not "centered."

d. There is nothing wrong with you, others, or the universe if you are not calm.

Relative to the past:

a. Happiness is not dependent on you being successful by any criteria.

b. Happiness is not dependent on you being contented with any state of the world. You may be *not unhappy* with the state of the world, and also wanting it to change.

Relative to the future:

a. Happiness is not dependent on there being a purpose to your life.

b. Happiness is not dependent on there being a calling to your life.

Happiness Is *Not* Fulfilling
a Cultural Value

This commentary represents the editor's synthesis of ideas Bruce Di Marsico expressed only in fragments.

M ANY cultures propose primary cultural values. For example:

* Freedom
* Harmony
* Being Loving
* Being Successful
* Having Self-discipline
* Intelligence
* Being Spiritual
* Politeness

Within a particular culture, these ideas are often spoken of as equivalent to happiness.

They are not. They are proposed to be qualities such that, if perfectly achieved, will bring happiness. This is most likely because important figures in the creation of the culture found that these qualities helped them get what they wanted, and were happy on that basis, and proposed that these qualities could help anyone and everyone get what they wanted.

As a happy person, you may be attracted to any of these qualities; happiness, though, is the taste in your own mouth. There can only be *your* happiness, and that can take any form whatsoever. Only you know.

PART III:

Unhappiness

SECTION I

What Is Unhappiness?

Defining Unhappiness

THERE are four basic definitions of unhappiness:
Most summarily, (1) unhappiness is believing you are not free. And why are you not free? Because in your freedom, (2) you believe you would be against yourself. More specifically, the way you believe you are against yourself is (3) you believe it would be wrong to have the feelings you like. Ultimately, (4) unhappiness is the belief in the wrongness of being: that your actions or feelings or the world could be wrong.

Unhappiness is believing that you are not free:

> Unhappiness is the belief that you are not free.
>
> FROM DECEMBER 5, 1987 LECTURE

> Unhappiness is the belief that you'll be sorry if you're free.
>
> FROM DECEMBER 5, 1987 LECTURE

> Unhappiness is believing that something is necessary, something has to be, should be, ought to be, or must be other than what it is.
>
> FROM WRITING: "THE CAUSE OF UNHAPPINESS"

> We simply won't, can't or want to be anything other than ourselves. And unhappiness is believing, none the less, that we ought to, that we should.
>
> FROM NOVEMBER 11, 1995 LECTURE

> Unhappiness is, itself, believing that something is necessary.
>
> FROM WRITING: "UNUM NECESSARIUM"

Unhappiness is believing that you are against yourself:

Unhappiness is believing that you are against yourself.
FROM WRITING: "ONE TRUTH"

Unhappiness is believing you know you are bad for yourself.
FROM WRITING: "YOU CAN BE HAPPY"

The belief in unhappiness is the belief in being wrong for oneself.
FROM WRITING: "YOU CAN BE HAPPY"

Unhappiness is certainly the fear that you don't act on your own behalf.
FROM NOVEMBER 11, 1995 LECTURE

Unhappiness is believing that something means you are against yourself.
FROM WRITING: "ONE TRUTH"

Unhappiness is believing that something you want or not means you are against yourself.
FROM WRITING: "ONE TRUTH"

Unhappiness is believing that you are not the way you should be.
FROM WRITING: "ONE TRUTH"

All unhappiness is the fear that we have a bad attitude for ourselves.
FROM WRITING: "THE CAUSE OF UNHAPPINESS"

Unhappiness is just a secularized belief in sinfulness, wrongness, and is the same as believing that we choose what we know to be wrong or bad for us.
FROM WRITING: "THE CAUSE OF UNHAPPINESS"

Unhappiness is believing it would be wrong to have the feelings we like.

Unhappiness is believing we have to forbid ourselves the feelings we like.
FROM WRITING: "THE TWO PRINCIPLES"

Unhappiness is believing (doubting, hesitating to believe) that we don't automatically choose to feel the way we most want and like best for us.
FROM WRITING: "SINCE PEOPLE BELIEVE"

You could say, unhappiness is a term for the feelings that people have about things that they believe they need to stop in order to feel good.
FROM WRITING: "YOU CAN BE HAPPY"

Unhappiness is any form of believing that when we don't get what we want, it means we are going to feel a way we don't want.
FROM WRITING: "THE CREATION OF THE OPTION METHOD"

Unhappiness, ultimately:

Unhappiness is the belief in the wrongness of being.
FROM WRITING: "YOU CAN BE HAPPY"

All Unhappiness Is a Matter of Belief

ALL unhappiness is a matter of belief.

All symptoms, expressions, feelings, thoughts, etc. that are unhappy are natural phenomena resulting from the belief of unhappiness.

Unhappiness is just the belief that there is, or was, or will be, something to be unhappy about.

Unhappiness is believing, thinking, feeling, sensing, that there is something for me to worry about, feel bad about, something to fear, something to be ashamed of, something about me for others to be unhappy about, etc.

Unhappiness is believing there is something wrong with me, something about me for me or others to be unhappy about.

Unhappiness is believing that there is something in me to cause unhappiness for me or others.

Unhappiness is believing that I am cursed.

Unhappiness is believing that there is something in me which will prevent me from ever being happy.

Unhappiness is believing that there is something in me which will not allow me to be always happy.

Unhappiness is believing that there is a serious defect or imperfection in me that prevents Perfect Happiness.

Unhappiness is believing that something about me will bring about my doom.

Unhappiness is believing that something in me will be my undoing.

Unhappiness is believing that my best intentions are tainted and are not really good intentions.

Unhappiness is believing that unhappiness is natural under some circumstances.

Unhappiness is believing that unhappiness is natural under all circumstances.

Unhappiness is believing I am bad for me.

Unhappiness is believing some things or people are bad for me and can make me be what I don't want to be.

Unhappiness is believing that I could become a person I don't want to be.

Unhappiness is believing that I could want, against my will, what could make me unhappy against my will.

Unhappiness is believing that I could believe, without my choice, what would make me unhappy.

Unhappiness is believing that I could accidentally cause myself to be unhappy.

Unhappiness is believing that things that I say or feel or think or do because I was unhappy, are things to be unhappy about.

Unhappiness is feeling that things I accidentally do that I don't like, are things I have to be unhappy about in order to prevent in the future.

Unhappiness is believing that accidents are proof there is something self-defeating or wrong with me.

Unhappiness is believing that anything I do that I don't like anymore after I do it is proof that there is something wrong with me.

Unhappiness is believing in evil.

Unhappiness is believing that something real called unhappiness exists apart from the belief in it.

Unhappiness is believing there is any more to unhappiness besides the belief that it could exist or happen.

Unhappiness is the belief that any physical sensation or feeling as such (without judgments or labels) may not be natural or real.

Unhappiness is believing that natural physical sensations should not be there.

The Fundamental Insight
of The Option Method

UNHAPPINESS is only a *belief*.

You are unhappy only because you *believe* it is natural for you to be.

You get unhappy only because you *believe* it is natural for you to get unhappy.

What you are unhappy about does not have the power to make you unhappy. You are unhappy only because you *believe* it does.

You are unhappy, not because you have to be, but only because you *believe* you must be.

You don't have to be unhappy. You only *believe* you do.

Being Kind to Yourself

THERE is no mystery about unhappiness. What you're afraid of is that it *is* mysterious, and that's why you experience it that way. You could be believing that it's all too simple, it's too good to be true, and so therefore, even though you've worked through something and you're no longer unhappy about it—oh, but you *know* yourself! That's already your own belief that you have to be unhappy, or that you will fail yourself if you are not unhappy, or that you can't keep a single straight thought in your body.

The Option Method never, ever implies anything. When we ask somebody, "Why are you unhappy?" or "What about that are you unhappy about?" we really want an answer, whatever the real answer is. But we *only* want an answer. We're never saying, "Why the hell are you unhappy?" That will, of course, never help anybody who thinks that themselves already

When you're using The Option Method wrongly for yourself, you're not as kind to yourself as you would be for someone else. When you keep repeating your unhappiness and you find yourself unhappy, what you're saying to yourself is "Why the hell am I unhappy about this again?" You're not good natured about it and you're not forgiving; you're not understanding like you would be for someone else.

There's a real reason you are unhappy. You're not out to screw yourself. You're not out to hurt yourself. You didn't wake up in the morning saying, "I think I'll drive a nail through my head!" You never set out to be unhappy. You thought somehow, in some way there was good reason and it was necessary for you to get unhappy.

Those people who have had experience with some versions of The Option Method may have learned something about not having to be unhappy about something. But also, every time they looked at their behavior they thought they were unhappy and they judged it. When they were unhappy and didn't want to be, and had no reason to be, they then said to themselves, "Why the hell are you unhappy again?"

Unhappiness Is for Future Happiness

January 19, 1976

THE only cause of unhappiness and dissatisfaction is the belief that we can (or will) feel more of what we want in the future rather than now.

We believe we will become more of what we want, more ourselves. We believe that this will make the future happier.

The belief is that what we are now feeling is not perfect and the happier, most natural way to be.

If we "try" to be happier than we are, or are really going to be, about something, we will feel dissatisfied now and disappointed later.

If we "play it cool" or "play it up" in order to boost our future happiness, we will feel unsettled now. Any distortion of "now" is to "improve" the future; it is supposed to work, but it doesn't.

We even deny what we want so that we will be surprised when we get it (if we get it).

We dis-enjoy the present in order to enjoy the future better.

The future can never be better; only *now* can!

What is happening now need not be better. It is what it is. We are where we are.

Desiring changes is a present experience. It is only dissatisfying when we don't enjoy it.

We don't enjoy our desires (or any other "now" experience) because we judge and evaluate them as if they were not desirable in order to "more enjoy" the future.

We dis-enjoy our desires by doubting if they will be fulfilled or by believing we will be happier after they are fulfilled.

If we believe that our desires are "no good" unless they are fulfilled, we will not enjoy them now. We will suspend or hold back until we foresee their satisfaction.

Holding back happiness now is a mistake. We do not enjoy the future because of *that*, any more than we are enjoying the present.

SECTION II

The Myth of Unhappiness

Nothing Is "Good" or "Bad" for Happiness

NOTHING is good and nothing is bad. Because everything is good if nothing is bad. A knife is bad for use as a hammer. A hammer is not good to use as a wrench. Different things are good for different things. An education is good for certain kinds of success. Certain kinds of education are bad for certain kinds of success. So things in the real world are good *for* things and bad *for* things.

And that "for" or "with" goes together with the "good" or "bad." Nothing is bad by itself. It's bad *for* something. Things are bad? That just means bad for your happiness or bad for your eternal soul. When a thing is assumed to be bad in a moral sense it means bad for your eternal soul or it doesn't have much meaning. And that means, in the long run, you're going to wind up unhappy. That's what bad means. That's what "sin" means, if sin has any meaning. And without anything connected to it, it has really no meaning.

You are really thinking that bad means bad for your happiness. But nothing can be bad for your happiness, but you can believe it to be so. And I don't want to say, "Unless you believe it's bad for your happiness." Because nothing is bad for your happiness, period. Nothing is bad for your happiness but you can believe that things are. And that's all. But you don't realize that all the time. The more you realize it the more you will make it pertinent and relevant to yourself.

And it can be lots of fun to do that. It'll never be a form of disgrace or shame or embarrassment or suffering or effort to go through that wonderful experience of finding out that you were believing you need to do something that you didn't need to. You didn't *need* to go to that wedding anyway. You never *had* to pay that anyway. To find out you thought you needed to do something and you didn't need to, is a wonderful freedom. To think that you weren't allowed something and to find out that you were is a wonderful feeling.

That's all we're talking about. Happiness. Nobody can make you happy. I don't know if anybody wants to. But if somebody wanted to, I think that it would just fit among those characteristics of things that they want. And I don't know if they know what your happiness is. But if that's what they want then they're going to be working for what they want. But the actual happiness that will ever exist for you will only be the one you want. Not the one that someone else wants for you. And if you're waiting for something astounding to happen to make you happy and stop being unhappy—then you believe you have to be unhappy.

I judge everything I feel like judging. I judge things to death. I judge the hell out of things. I like that movie. I didn't like that directing. I liked the color. I didn't like that costume. I judge whatever I want to judge. And I enjoy it. Why not? What am I doing wrong? I'm enjoying myself. That's got nothing to do with unhappiness. Unhappiness would be sitting next to the lady who says to me, "Shhh." And believing, "Oh, I'm sorry; I shouldn't have said that." And believing that I shouldn't be judging all these things and not out loud, certainly. The only unhappiness is to believe you shouldn't be judging.

But who's going to say, "I think I'll feel bad about this, and I think that's something to be disgusted by, and I think this is something to be angry about," if they know they're going to pay the price for those judgments that way?

I will judge a thing on its terms. But not on whether it has the power to make me unhappy or not. It doesn't. Because that's not a judgment. That's a lie. See, a person who wants to be happy doesn't go around conferring goodness on things. You know, this is good. This is something not to be unhappy about. This is good. This is not bad. Where the hell do you get off? These things were all good long before you came on this planet. The only thing you're going to do is *admit* they're good.

Myths of Unhappiness

January 7, 1975

THE belief that the good and beautiful things that we want or have are good because they ward off or strengthen us against "unhappiness" is the cause of unhappiness.

The truth is that all desires, and the desirability of things or circumstances, come from our happiness.

Conversely, those things and feelings which we don't desire, and those lacks of desire, also come from our happiness. In short, our recognition of what we want or don't want comes from our happiness, not as a need to avoid "unhappiness."

Unhappiness doesn't exist. It isn't real. It seems to exist as a result of a simple belief and the subsequent beliefs that naturally follow from that belief.

1. I can be "unhappy." "Unhappiness" exists and can happen to me naturally. Historically, this was proposed as "evil" exists and can happen to me.
2. Maybe I will be unhappy. I want to avoid "unhappiness." Maybe I can avoid it. Maybe I can strengthen myself against it, or insure against it.
3. Happiness is a way of avoiding unhappiness. I can be happy (safely) if I do what will protect against unhappiness.

    There are "right and wrong" ways of doing this. Getting what I want will protect me from unhappiness. If I want the "right" things, I will be glad if I get the "right" things.

    This is the distinction of good vs. bad in "Good" wanting, thinking, having, etc. vs. "Bad" wanting, thinking, having, doing, etc.
4. If I want what I should want and if I have what I should want and if I behave (interiorly and exteriorly) as I should, I will be happy.
5. The reverse of the above is also held as true. If I don't want, have, behave as I should, I will become unhappy.

Therefore:

6. I must always be and have what I need in order to avoid unhappiness.

    And then there is the intervening experience of life's "truth": "I do not have the power to get or keep what I need to avoid all unhappiness."

    The real truth of life is: There is no need to avoid "unhappiness."

    There is, of course, never enough power to avoid what only exists in one's beliefs, as long as the belief is constantly carried, held, presented and given the existence of an absolute truth in one's mind.

Therefore:

7. Some unhappiness is inevitable and natural, but power and a strong personality (virtue in the old Roman-Greek-Hebrew sense) can go far in warding off much unhappiness, but only if I am vigilant about my desires and the direction they take me.

8. The fear of unhappiness is the same as the fear of losing or not maintaining the power and virtue necessary to avoid unhappiness.

    Life's experience shows that it takes "time" to acquire the strengths and protections needed, both 'things' in the world and in the personality. Love relationships are the perfect model of combining the need for control over the world and one's personality since it is believed that only by control over one's own personality can one earn the "good" personality of the beloved.

    Perfectly satisfying sex would be the reward of doing and being the "right" way, which is the best way of eliciting the "'right" responses from one's partner which is mutually satisfying (i.e., each "making" the other happy, therefore each making themselves happy in the "best" way, which is to be most satisfying to the other, etc.).

9. Since I am not perfectly happy I cannot believe that I can ever know or be certain of what is the "best" to be or have. I can only hope that in time, I can get better, happier, more self-confident—more protected.

10. I cannot trust that all my desires will lead me to greater insurance against unhappiness. I will not trust that all my desires can perfectly lead me into the perfect avoidance of unhappiness.
    Even my greatest joys must be hesitant or else I will be carried away

to what might not give me the protection I need against unhappiness. I may find myself self-abandoning to joy and pleasure and great happiness, leaving myself unguarded, unarmed, and unprepared for life after these joys end. I will have tasted joy by dropping fear, which was my only protection against unhappiness.

My desires which promise the greatest happiness rewards are only good if they are what I should want and what I can believe will produce the benefits that they should.

Unbridled sexual desires are therefore the epitome of one's self-deceit and carelessness.

If I am to have careless sex then it must not be with someone I want to avoid unhappiness with, namely my beloved or my spouse. I don't want to mislead us into believing we can trust each other's every desire. I know I don't want my beloved to trust me more than I should be trusted.

11. We are all somewhat misled and misleading.

Authoritative and authoritarian systems of belief (Philosophy, Theology, Religion, Psychology) become very attractive. They propose more success if we "connect" our values and beliefs to those of these systems. Since they all propose it is good to have fear and unhappiness as a way of avoiding greater unhappiness none will ever succeed.

Unsuccessful (in the sense of deprived of the fruits of the system or punished by the system) members of such systems (Political, Social, Religious, etc.) will find self-determination and personal freedom, reactionary doing-my-own-thing, I'm my own God-guide, a more attractive alternative to the system.

This appeal is also very negative and based on fear: "I may not do much better but at least I will not be misled by another's self-deception that they know the right way."

12. There is one "right" way" or "There is no right way, there is just some belief system derived from one of these previously listed beliefs, which usually amounts to 'doing one's best,' or 'following the Inner God' through evolution, etc. These Inner Gods of course also believe that unhappiness can and does exist."

13. a. This is taught by Inner or Outer Gods: one should not do everything one wants; only what one should want.
b. One should be what one believes one should be.

(I replaced "I" with "one" to show how these beliefs shift from personal experience and advice to becoming points of view and absolute truths through which we see ourselves and the universe: thereby completing the self-alienation process).

14. The "good" things I want such as health and friendship, comfort, pleasure, and happiness, etc. are good because they serve for avoiding unhappiness.

15. Happiness is the servant means of avoiding unhappiness.

Happiness is not "good" in itself (as indeed nothing is) but only insofar as it helps me to avoid the devil. Oops! I mean unhappiness.

Happiness and my desire for it are good (and holy) only insofar as they protect me from unhappiness (and evil) and help me get what is right to have, in order to avoid unhappiness.

Happiness and my wanting are only good if they help me get what I need.

Happiness and my wanting are only good if they can help to avoid unhappiness, otherwise they deceive.

My happiness and my desires are only good if I can see them produce what I should feel and have.

There Is No Cause of Unhappiness

August 22, 1975

NOTHING makes or causes people to believe that they can be unhappy. They think that something does. They deduce that it is true. They never believed that they don't have to believe that they can be unhappy. They simply believed it in the absence of another belief. The other belief is that "No one can cause unhappiness. Happiness is the cause of all."

Nothing caused the first belief except that happiness did not yet act to bring the new belief. Happiness brings the cure of the absence of its manifestation.

There is no cause of unhappiness or not getting what we want or not believing. There is a "cure."

There is no cause of darkness but there can be light. If any ask why there is darkness, darkness remains for them. If any ask for light, then when light comes and "removes" or "cures" the darkness, then we can see what the light came for us to see. The darkness was for the light to enlighten. Nothing causes your not believing, not feeling, not knowing and all the not wanted feelings, thoughts, behavior and events that follow from the not yet believing or knowing or being aware.

Nothing causes ignorance. It is still, though, not the natural state. It is the emptiness to be filled by knowledge.

Nothing causes unhappiness. Happiness is the natural state of man. Happiness coming is the cause of the desire for happiness to come. Want more and more. All that you are and have is for happiness to change you. Let it. Want it. Be glad when it does.

Want opportunities to be glad for. Be glad to have opportunities to be glad. Expect happiness to manifest itself. Love it, encourage it, want it, be glad when it does, and ask for more when you want to ask for more.

SECTION III

Unhappiness as a Motivator

More About How Unhappiness Happens

November 11, 1995

So we've got the basic fundamentals down; fear, unhappiness, learned judgments, emotions, and events. There are a few other kinds of insights that I'll be glad to share with you as they come up.

When a person learns that they don't have to be unhappy about something, that usually has a resounding effect, like dominoes. You find that you don't have to be unhappy about one thing and that carries with it a whole bunch of other things that, all of a sudden, for some reason, you realize you don't have to be unhappy about anymore.

You didn't look at your beliefs about them, but you're not unhappy about them anymore because somehow we peeled the onion and in uncovering why you're unhappy about [something else] you have probably touched on a number of things that you also had that rationale about.

So "dead cousins" probably applies also to dead mothers and fathers and sisters and brothers and dead pets; things like that, if you deal with that as an unhappiness.

Now there are other things. One of the things we know about people, since we know these are all choices, is that people are always doing what they *want* to do. Some people believe that they're doing what they should do, but that's still what they want to do. Some people believe they're doing what they shouldn't do, but they're still wanting to do it. So in either case all people are always doing what they want to do.

All people in all cases are always doing what they want to do and never *not*. If someone else is actually doing it—if somebody tied your hands up and are pulling them with cords—okay, we won't blame you for that.

But insofar as *you're* doing it, you're wanting to do it, even though you don't believe you're wanting to. So people might say to me, "I don't want to go to work today, but I have to," that's what they may say. They may even think they believe it, but the exact opposite is the truth.

The truth is that they want to go to work and they don't have to. See, because the same truth is true for everybody. Nobody has to do anything. They don't have to. Nobody can make them go to work. If you refuse to go to work, you're not going to work, right? You don't have to go to work. You can stay home and take the consequences. You don't have to go to work.

So anybody who says they have to go to work is not telling the truth and that they say they'd really rather stay home is not telling the truth. The truth is they want to go to work because they want to get paid. They want to go to work for reasons that they have.

Now people don't just like to go to work just for the hell of going to work. There are very few jobs that engender that enthusiasm and certainly the people I talk to when they say they don't want to go to work, but they have to, they're talking about just the opposite of what I'm talking about.

The truth is they don't have to go to work, but they want to. And what do you think they're going to do? They're going to go to work because they want to, not because they have to. They're going to work in spite of the fact that they believe they have to because they have reasons—there are reasons why they want to and that is: they don't want to get fired, they want to have a good reputation with their boss, they want to collect their pay.

They don't want the consequences of not going to work. The same reasons people have for paying taxes. Everybody will say they don't want to pay their taxes, but they have to. I don't know anybody who doesn't want to pay their taxes and who wants the government on their back.

People want to pay their taxes for the same reasons. They don't want the consequences of not paying their taxes. All right, maybe they don't want to pay every penny, but they want to pay a believable tax and fill out a believable tax form. And they could tell you that they hate doing this on April 15th or whenever it is, but they want to.

People are always doing what they want to even though they describe it as not what they want to do, even the so-called disgusting things that they steel up the courage to do. It's because they really believe that, all things equal, they want to do this.

They'd rather give mouth-to-mouth to this person than to see them die, etc. Something like that. Or eat this food that a foreigner eats, which they've never considered food before and to them has never been thought of as food, like say lamb's eyeballs.

They'd have to see and they'd have to believe that it won't hurt them and that they want to be hospitable and gracious to their host or they want to be gracious to their hospitable host and they might in fact steel up the courage to do it, but they can only do it by wanting to. They can't do it by believing they have to or they should. The only way they can want to is to change their beliefs about it from non-food to food. They don't have to believe it's delicious, but they can't believe that it's abominable. You see?

But changing of beliefs is how we acculturate. We can be brought as six-year-olds to a foreign country and become one of them. We can be taught at 12 years old and become one of them. At about 13, probably not. That's only because we've already decided we're not going to allow more acculturation. We say we've had it with acculturation. I'm only going to become as learned as I want to be and only in the areas that I want to be.

But in the earlier stages we're willing to be persuaded that it's for our good, for our general good even if we can't spell it out. That's how we adapt our morality. That's the way we started believing that things were bad, even if we didn't understand how or why, we understood one thing: it was for our good that we did.

We knew that if we didn't we'd get something like "You don't believe that's bad?" and get some condemnation for not believing it's bad, even if we had no reason to believe it's bad. We knew we were at least expected to believe it was bad or to pretend we knew why it was bad.

So, we acculturate and only by changing our beliefs can we ever change our behaviors. But in The Option Method we're not here to help people eat lamb's eyeballs or spiders for that matter, but just not to be disgusted at the possibility if they don't want to be if they're going to be at a banquet at the embassy. It would be nice if they didn't vomit on the diplomats or any other person who eats in a way that's foreign to them.

Unhappiness is the fear of happiness because that's obvious. You never had to be unhappy about anything and yet you thought it was a good idea.

Whenever you were unhappy in your life you thought that somehow, "Oh, that makes sense." Well, why did it make sense? Because being happy was abominable and that's what we find out when we ask a person what are they afraid of if they're not unhappy.

If they were happy that would be abominable. And by abominable what I mean is the worst possible way of existence, that it would mean that you loved what you hated and you hated what you loved and you liked what you didn't like and you didn't like what you did like and you wanted what you didn't want and you didn't want what you really did want.

That it could mean all that to just not be unhappy. That you were an insane monkey and you weren't far wrong because all people somehow resemble insane monkeys.

They operate apparently without much rhyme or reason and very quickly on the unhappy side. You can't trick people into being happy very easily, but you can trick them into being unhappy real easily. "Boo!" Most people reject and repulse, etc., and draw back.

So it can be fairly said that human beings have quite an affinity toward unhappiness. They've long believed in its value and they've long believed in its help. They've long turned to it for help. So it's not strange that anybody should have trouble not being unhappy. They'd be almost quite unnatural.

But once we know what it's based on, the dynamics behind the unhappiness are just very simple. Well, then we can question. Are you really afraid this would happen if you weren't unhappy? Couldn't you act unhappy? Would you have to really be unhappy? If you really think that's the only way of getting out of this hell hole, why couldn't you just sputter and stammer and spit and foam. Couldn't you act that out? Is there no saliva in you?

If you must act unhappy, act unhappy. If you're about to be attacked and you think that acting unhappy is going to really help, can't you throw up on your rapist? They won't want to have anything to do with you.

No one has to actually be unhappy. Any case for unhappiness is merely that, an attempt to make a case for unhappiness, because all you're saying is "This is what I want to achieve, this is what I want to get" and you can have that.

You do the unhappiness in order to get the thing that you want so that you won't be unhappy. That's pretty much like taking your head and throwing it down the block and then saying "Excuse me, I've got to go down the block and get my head."

You're making yourself feel that you need something in order to have the right to go get it. When we turn it around and ask people what are they afraid of if they're not unhappy, is that you're taking away my justification for doing what I want. I'm going to be left with my mere selfish self that says I want this, I want that, I want this, I want that. I have no precedence and I have no support.

But unhappiness, hey, it makes me unhappy. Nobody questions. I can have that ice cream cone before dinner. But the Good Humor truck is here, but the Good Humor truck is here. I saw my cousins do that, my nephews do that. They were perfectly happy and the Good Humor truck came before dinner in the neighborhood.

The Good Humor truck in New Jersey is an ice cream truck. He comes around with ice cream on a stick and stuff like that. These people who are old enough to know decided that to act unhappy might very well work and it does.

So unhappiness tends to then get looked at as if it's being used as a tool. I myself, although I have seen it continuously, don't believe it. I don't believe that people use unhappiness as a tool. I believe that people believe they're going to get unhappy. In fact I know that. They believe they're going to get unhappy and what they're using as a tool is letting you see it, the decision of whether to show it to you or not, whether to demonstrate their unhappiness in whatever form and how badly they need to do that.

Or else we're just talking about faking and that's fine. Then we're not talking about unhappiness. Pretending to be unhappy is just that and that's what I started with.

So since people can pretend to be unhappy and we've done that as children, we didn't ever have to really be unhappy, did we, in order to get what we wanted? The only thing that being unhappy does is keeps us from being happy. It punishes us. When we're unhappy, in effect we've punished ourselves. We've kept ourselves from being happy.

So it must be maybe that we believe that we ought to do that. It's not some small thing that's going on, except for those areas where you think you can afford it, but that we know is a big danger. It's a slippery slope because once you think you can afford a little unhappiness, before you know it you're taking it in by the gallon.

"Shoulds" Have No Value

Do I need any protection to not do things that I don't want to do? Do I need to be held in restraint from not doing things that I don't want to do? Do I need a *should* for any reason whatsoever? Do I need a *should* to tell me to do something I want to do? No, I already want to do it. Do I want a *should* to tell me to do something I don't want to do? No, thank you. So what value are any *shoulds* in my life (to tell myself that I should this or I should that)? I don't really even value *shoulds* because with things that I love, I don't need to believe I should. And things that I don't want, I don't want to know that I should. It's really only another way of saying I don't want to.

If we really believe we should do something, you know psychologically what happens in our bodies? Our bodies believe us, and start acting like we don't want to do it. You see because what you've told your body was "I wouldn't want to do this in a million years, I just think I should." And your body says, okay, and now acts like you wouldn't want to do it in a million years.

So once you believe you should go on a diet, you should lose weight, gain weight, anything else, forget it. Your body will obey you. We've got this "unfortunate" relationship with our body: it believes us, and anything we believe, it believes. And if we believe we should do something, we have effectively taught our self that we don't want to. If you believe you should put on seat belts, you're believing you don't want to. If you're believing you should eat your spinach, you're believing you don't want to eat spinach—or else what are you talking about? If you're not trying to tell yourself you don't want to, what are you telling yourself?

So, it's no mystery why "shoulds" would undermine and make us unhappy. We are telling ourselves that we should and believing that it has more validity than our wants. We think that we can make ourselves do what we want by telling ourselves that's what we *should* do, to reinforce our desires. And that's really a way of telling ourselves we don't want to.

All "Shoulds" Are Beliefs

ALL *shoulds* are beliefs of what to do, feel, say, think, believe, know, want, have, be, etc. in order to avoid unhappiness, e.g., "I should want this if I am taking care of myself." All doing of what is "right" is to avoid unhappiness.

"After I do what I should, then I am allowed to then be happy." *Should* is a way of earning freedom from worry and unhappiness. This is *called* happiness, but it is really the peace of relief of "natural unhappiness" (which is believed inevitable if one doesn't earn the right to avoid it).

If I do what I should do, then I don't have to be unhappy. Then I have escaped the obligation of being unhappy. "Unhappiness comes from doing what I want unless I can believe I *should* do that which I want." "Unhappiness comes from getting what I want unless I can believe I should have it."

*Should*s are derived from having a wanting that is not a *should*, from a place where there was no previous *should*. It is thought that without a *should*, that wanting must be avoided and the opposite is what should be wanted—attended to.

What one *should* want is derived as opposite to what one *should not* want.

"You should not want to do everything you want." Therefore: "You should want only some wants which follow what you should want."

"In order to avoid unhappiness I should love you and be with you and learn from you, etc. But I am still unhappy." I realize it is because of my above belief that I can complicate matters by becoming self-reflexive: I believe I should not have *should*s. Now I believe that in order to avoid unhappiness, I should not want you just because I should want you. Now in order to avoid unhappiness, I should not be with you just in order to avoid unhappiness.

Happiness Is Freedom

THERE are all those words that are substitutes for being unhappy: you should, you ought to, you're supposed to—all the contraries to freedom. They're equal to unhappiness. If you believe there's anything that you're supposed to do, there's anything you should do—if you believe you ought to visit your grandchildren, that you're supposed to call your mother, if you believe you should pay the rent and you ought to pay your taxes, etcetera—you're going to be unhappy. You're going to feel a lot of pressure and a lot of stress. Because you're piling up "shoulds" against "shoulds" and "supposed to's" against "supposed to's."

As you know, I used to live that life. What school should I go to? What classes should I take? What teachers should I sign up for? What fraternities should I join? What sports will I be able to be good at? And we go through life somewhat confused. Everything is a "should" weighed against another "should." So we seek smarter friends and wiser counselors, who have their own "shoulds" and "supposed to's" and "ought to's" and "need to's." All of which will make them unhappy. So believing in, there's anything that you need to do, will make you unhappy. Anything you should do; that'll make you unhappy. Anything you're supposed to clear up; that'll make you unhappy. Anybody you have to save; that'll make you unhappy. Anybody you ought to love; that'll really make you unhappy.

All the shoulds, ought to's, supposed to's have no real article with them. "Should" has a meaning in English. You should use this for that. If you want to get this, you're supposed to do that. They are formulas with a beginning and an end. Not "You're supposed to shut up." "You're supposed to be wise." "You're supposed to be rich." If these words have any real meanings there's an article attached to them and a preposition, as in *good for* and *bad for*. *Good* and *bad* do not exist on their own.

On Owing and Debts, and Freedom, Forgiveness, and Gifts

June 12, 1993

Charity

One does not have charity (gracious love) *toward* another. One has charity, or not, in oneself, as oneself.

Charity is an attitude, a characteristic of the possessor; not a garment to be displayed, or a performance to be given for someone. Charity is not an action or a behavior, albeit sincere.

The concept of turning the other cheek, or walking the extra mile, is charity, not because the acts are a kindness to another (who knows if they are?), but because they come from an attitude of peace and happiness that is free to see the other as not frightening or not owed these freely given gifts.

Gifts, in order to be gifts, are precisely *not owed*. Otherwise, they would be payment of debts.

Charity (*xaris* or *xarisma*) means free, gratis, grace, a gift of freedom for the one who possesses it. He or she who possessed this grace was seen as charismatic, inward qualities shining out attractively and noticed by others. This was sometimes portrayed in art as a halo or an aura. By extension it meant to the Greeks (and Christian Greeks) comeliness, beauty, loveliness, lovingness, etc. In all cases it was known as the quality of the gifted one, not as it might be expressed to another in gifts to them.

Not as the modern notion of *giving, giving, giving*. That is exactly what the unloving would want it to mean; for others who are charitable to give to them. Since when is any grace defined by those who do not have it? Those without charity are the least competent to define it—and the most likely to define it as another's giving. The truly charitable do not presume to define it for others; they just are free and expressively grateful.

Giving to the poor is not charity because the poor are needy or deserving, but because the giver is free to give whatever they give, in fact, the giver may be as poor as the poor they give to. There is no reward for charity became it is not a task or an earning work. It is like throwing fish into the sea. What is the reward? It is more like a laugh, a smile, a song. It is an inward state that seems to be expressed, and others may notice, sometimes because they are the recipient (dare I say, inadvertently, by time and circumstance) of the grateful expression. Certainly giving to the poor, or otherwise taking care of the needy, is not notable for what is done. The "contribution" is infinitesimal to the whole body of possibilities.

The person with charity feels grateful. Only they know what form that gratitude takes. If they give, it is from that gratefulness, not because the other "needs" or deserves something from them. Ultimately defined, charity means nothing if not happiness in the individual. Expressions of so-called charity mean nothing like charity unless they come from freely, happily, choosing one's own expression of joy.

No One Owes Anyone Anything

If I can have no more than what I can get (and keep) by myself, then no one is to blame. There is nothing that anyone should do for me. If I trust another, then that is my choice. They do not owe me to perform or deliver for me, or be as good for me as I believe I would be for me. Neither do they owe me to be as good for me as I think they should. Each person can only act as he believes is best for himself.

Happiness is releasing the world from its so-called obligations to me. Nothing and no one is supposed to be better for me, or is supposed to be in any way different than what it is.

This is true forgiveness: there is nothing to forgive because there are no debts, nothing that any should do for me.

To be really happy; forgive everyone for everything in the past, present and future. They have done, are doing, and will do all they can; the best they know how.

SECTION IV

Facets of Unhappiness

Supposed to Be

I AM supposed to be . . .
You are supposed to be . . .
They are supposed to be . . .
Life is supposed to be . . .
The world is supposed to be . . .
God is supposed to be . . .
I am supposed to be good at . . .

For example: I am supposed to be good at getting loved. If I'm not, something is wrong with me.

Or another example: I should be good at getting what is most important to me. If I don't do what it takes, I am failing to take care of myself. Something is wrong with me.

These are all kinds of ways of meaning the same thing: I ought to . . . I should . . . etc.

Feeling badly is the same as feeling that "you are bad."

Feeling bad means, and is, your own feeling yourself as "bad," or feeling yourself as being what you should not be.

Feeling fear is feeling that you will have to be unhappy. It is how it feels to believe that in the future you will have to feel bad; that you will have to feel yourself as bad.

Bad means deserving of unhappiness, or not deserving happiness.

Feeling bad means:

You ought to or should feel that you are being a way you shouldn't be.

You ought to believe (or you do now believe) that you are not the way you should be.

"There's Something Wrong with You"

WE have discussed unhappiness in terms of chains and series of causes, "I am unhappy because of this, I am unhappy because of that." And we've gotten to understand that unhappiness is a chain of events, just as happiness is a chain of events. We've gotten to understand that we can analyze them and that our job as analysts would be just to analyze that chain of causes and effects. What I want to do tonight is to bring it full circle. I'm back to telling you that none of that is true, none of that is really where it's at, that that's not the way it is. There really isn't a whole series of chains and connections. There aren't really "the reason for this is the reason for that is the reason for this," but that is the way it seems to be. And I guess you know that too probably. All the things that we call reasons are really equivalent. Now, I'm unhappy because such and such a thing happened. I'm unhappy because this, I'm unhappy because that, but all of those *becauses*, in a sense, are just simply another kind of restating.

When someone stated "I'm unhappy, because, and I'm unhappy then, because . . .," they gave a reason. All right, that's true. Pragmatically speaking, it does make a difference for you to know the reasons. "I'm unhappy because I'm not comfortable, I'm sad because I'm unhappy." Though you know they're really meaning the same thing, pragmatically it makes a difference. So, then you fish around to get another kind of an answer to give you something to talk about, and you take that and ask "Why does that make you unhappy?" and the answer comes "That makes me unhappy because."

Now, I want to show you that those are also really equivalent, that all happiness and all the feelings about unhappiness are all the same, none of them are really very different from each other. We've often said that "I am okay" means the same as "I am happy." "I'm okay" means "I'm happy" means "well-being." So, we've got all kinds of equivalent terms for that: I'm where I want to be, doing what I want to do, I'm happy, I'm feeling what I want to feel. I'm joyous, I'm at peace. So, it is with unhappiness. Being unhappy, as we've often said and often seen, comes from the belief that I ought to be unhappy about something. That it's impossible to be unhappy without the belief that I ought to be unhappy.

We've always talked about the belief that I ought to be unhappy and unhappiness itself as cause and effect. I want to show you that they are really one and the same thing: I have said, "Your being unhappy comes from the belief that you ought to be unhappy"; let me now say that that being unhappy *is* that belief. Up until now, we've always talked about them, for pedagogical purposes, as one comes from the other. One *is* the other. Being unhappy doesn't *come* from the belief that I ought to be unhappy, it doesn't *come* from the belief that I must be unhappy or I should be unhappy, but it is *exactly* the same as the belief "I must be unhappy." We say, "Unhappy is because I don't get what I want" (and it really boils down to that no matter how we put it). Then we give all kinds of reasons for that. "I'm not getting what I want because I'm not wanting it enough, or I'm not unhappy enough or . . ."

It is not a "because." Unhappiness doesn't come from not getting what I want, but in a real sense it *is* not getting what I want. Being unhappy is not getting what I want. We could say, "What I want is to be happy, so being unhappy is not getting what I want, which is to be happy." And even though we may put all kinds of particulars in the way, like money or health or love, I'm unhappy that I'm not getting what I want. The reason why I want these is because I want happiness, and I think this will give it to me. But I want to show that they don't come from each other, that they are all the same thing. So, if I say I'm unhappy because I don't have money, I'm unhappy because I'm not loved, it's really not because of these. "I'm unhappy" is I am not getting what I want, which in this case is love or in this case is money or in this case is health. And unhappiness doesn't *come* from that, that *is* unhappiness.

"What I am unhappy *about* is that I am not getting what I want." That almost universally is accepted by anyone as what unhappiness means. Now, we're changing it to my unhappiness *is* the same thing as not getting what I want. But why is unhappiness the same thing as not getting what I want? Under what circumstances, how would it be really okay with us if we didn't get what we wanted? No one could know unhappiness about not getting what they wanted, if they didn't believe that they were the reason that they weren't getting what they wanted.

The only reason you can be unhappy is because you believe you're making yourself unhappy. You may have noticed anytime you have ever come to the conclusion that what you wanted really was impossible, you stopped being unhappy about it. When the dead were finally dead in your mind, you were no longer unhappy about the dead. When the job was finally lost and finally done, and there was no way back to that job, you were no longer unhappy about having been fired. If there is unhappiness at all after that, it's in reference to something else similar, where you may mess up and you are trying to prevent yourself from being at fault or of being the cause of that you are not getting what you want. The fear is of *your* being the cause of your not getting to what you want. *That* is what unhappiness is. Unhappiness doesn't come from that, it's what it *is*. I'm unhappy because I don't get what I want, but that would be okay if it wasn't my fault and truly not in my power. If I really saw and really believed that it was not in my power, I would not be unhappy that I didn't get what I want. There would be no need to motivate myself through unhappiness; there would be no sense in motivating myself through unhappiness.

And when we see that there is nothing to motivate ourselves for, we can't be unhappy. So, I want to make a new statement. To be unhappy, I have to believe I could have or should have made a difference. The facts prove somehow that you didn't make a difference. Why do we keep saying to ourselves, I must be unhappy or I should be unhappy or I ought to be unhappy? To motivate ourselves. Why do we want to motivate ourselves? Why do we talk about motivation? What is motivation? Why do we think we want to motivate ourselves towards something and for what? To be unhappy I have to believe I could or should have made a difference. The fact that I didn't make a difference proves that there must be something wrong with me. That awareness (I am hesitating to call it a belief) that there must be something wrong with me is unhappiness. Is the reason, the cause, the rationale, the motivation, the very essence of unhappiness. It is the thing that explains to me everything that I could ever need to know about why I didn't get what I wanted. It's the thing that explains to me why I am not who I want to be. It explains to me why I am not motivated. It explains to me why I am 5 feet behind where I want to be. It motivates me, but it also accounts for "I am not motivated" and it also accounts for "I need motivation," it also accounts for such a thing as motivation.

What is wanting? Wanting is just simply moving toward. We often say that we use wanting as a motivation, but it is the same thing as motivation. We made distinctions on motivations: there is wanting as a way to motivate yourself and needing is a way to motivate yourself, but what does motivating oneself mean? It means moving towards, mobilizing yourself. Why would you want to mobilize yourself? Somehow you believe you are not mobilizing yourself; somehow there is a question of mobilizing yourself. I'm asking myself, "Why I am not being mobilized?" Now, I can answer that in one or two ways. I mobilize myself because I want to or I need to. Why am I not being mobilized toward leaving this room? I don't want it enough or because I am needing to not. Why am I not understanding The Option Method? Why doesn't it live in my life? Why am I not happier than I am? Why am I less than happy? There must be something wrong with me, and I'll come up with all kinds of nice little nouns to explain it. I'm stupid, I'm sick, I need more time, I'm stubborn, I'm recalcitrant, I am confused, I am this, I am that, I am . . . —there's something wrong with me. And we have a whole constellation of vocabulary to explain that there must be something wrong with me. What's wrong with me? The belief is that there must be something wrong with me. But is it a belief or is it not indeed that there *is* something wrong with me?

There is awareness, an incontrovertible, undisputable awareness that there is something wrong with me. Whenever I want to know why I am not where I want to be, the very fact that I want to know it is because there is something wrong with me, and the very answer to the question is because there is something wrong with me. The reason for the question is because there is something wrong with me and the answer to the question is because there must be something wrong with me. And when I ask myself why am I not a happier person, my answer has to be, there must be something wrong with me. But then I say, well, why did I ask the question, why am I am not a happier person? That's because there must be something wrong with me. Well, why do I want to believe that there must be something wrong with me? There must be something wrong with me for wanting to believe there must be something wrong with me, because I know there is nothing wrong with me. So, there must be something wrong with me. And we constantly are facing this.

Ever since you were children when you didn't get what you wanted, you said to yourself pre-verbally, however you want to call it, there must be something wrong with me. You wanted to stay up, they'd put you to bed. I want to stay up; they are making me go to bed. There must be something wrong with me. I am hungry and they are not feeding me, there must be some reason why they are not feeding me. There must be something wrong with me. I don't want to eat the food they are trying to force down my throat. There must be something wrong with me. First of all, for not liking the food, second of all, for not being able to motivate them to not give it to me. How come I can't make my mother treat me nicer? There must be something wrong with me. How come I can't enjoy the way she is treating me? There must be something wrong with me. And every time I've never gotten what I wanted, there must be something wrong with me. That would explain it.

And so, ever since you were children, you wanted to believe, you have believed, you have been aware, there must be something wrong with you. And that all hinges on the concept that you should have made a difference, that you should have been able to have what you didn't have, and that there was a reason why you didn't have it and you were the reason. So and so doesn't love me. There must be something wrong with you that people don't love you. Oh, yes, if I were happier, people would love me more. That's what it is, that's what's wrong with me. So, you become a follower of The Option Method, and now you "know" what's wrong with you is that you are unhappy.

For wanting what I can't have, there must be something wrong with me. I want you to love me, you are not loving me. That presents me with a dilemma, either there is something wrong with you or there is something wrong with me. Let's say I go with "There is something wrong with you." But then, how come I can't make the difference? How come even though there is something wrong with you, my being the good person that I am has not made you change, at least in my case? Why haven't I been able to win you over? Why haven't I been able to cure you? Why haven't I been able to get your love?

I took a survey and I found that no one is God. And everybody I asked who they were, none of them were God. See, what's wrong with you is you become aware that you are not all-powerful. That you don't have the power to do everything. You know that, you are aware of it, you become aware of it as a child. What's wrong with me is I am not you, and I am not all there is and that I am not all-powerful. And if I can't get you to love me, there must be something wrong with me. If I can't get you to be happy, there must be something wrong with me, because I should be able to do that. Why do I think I should be able to do that? Because that's what I am trying to do.

The reason I believe I should be able to make my mother change me when I am wet, is because that's what I want. What do I mean by want? That's what I move toward. I move from wetness to dryness. I just move there and it doesn't happen, and I say why, why. Why doesn't it happen? Why haven't I moved? But I *am* moving, and I don't become aware of my own movement, that I am becoming happy.

It is very similar to this. You always constantly talk about your past as if it were present. You say "I'm the kind of person who'll"—even if you're not being that kind of person, right now. "I get unhappy when . . ." even if it's not occurring at that moment. You assume that you're back where you were, to account for why you are not where you want to be. Somehow you know you are moving somewhere. You are moving toward being more happy. You are, you are just simply moving toward being more well, being more yourself, being more whatever. And to account for why you are not where you are going, you say, "Of course, I am back there." It's like a person who is walking down a path and looks over their shoulder and says, "Why am I back there?" And he's not back there, what he means is "Why am I not over *there*?"

Tending toward goodness: some people talk about it as tending toward cosmicness, Cosmic Unity. It's what you are moving toward. Now, you can call that tending, wanting, needing, fearing, but still nonetheless tending. You are tending toward being happier. All of you tend toward being happier. You all tend to be happy, but when you don't get where you are going you say there must be a reason that you are not there yet. There's got to be another reason other than merely "I am not there yet." The reason is there is something wrong with me. And even if I wanted to instead go into, "There's something wrong with *you*," I have to assume that it shouldn't be that way. For example, if you don't love me, there's something wrong with you. Why is that wrong? Why shouldn't it be that way? What is it I am tending toward? I am tending toward your being happy. I am becoming "you being happy." I am becoming, I am wanting to be, I am moving toward everything being okay, including you, it and everything.

You could walk down a street, you could see two people fighting, two other people fighting across the street and you will have the instinctive reaction that there must be something wrong with you. Allow yourself to get in touch with that. You can pick up a newspaper and read about something happening in Southeast Asia and say, there must be something wrong with me. When even objectively, it has absolutely nothing to do with you, it would seem. And yet you could say there must be something wrong with me that those two people are fighting and I am not doing anything about it.

Someone told me that the other day: There must be something wrong with me that the people are starving. And then, you could even become a little more insightful and realize you *know* what's wrong with you. There must be something wrong with you to believe that there must be something wrong with you.

You could reach the level of insight that says, "There must be something wrong with me for not being happy. For not being there." You recognize that you are not all-powerful, and that you are not there. Since you are tending to be there, since everything in your nature is moving toward being there, you know that, you are aware of that. "That's what I move toward, that's what I am moving toward." Somehow you ask yourself "Why am I not changing. I sense that I want to change myself, or change it, or change them, or change everything, or change anything I want to change." And at that very moment, you *are* changing; I have asked myself why am I not changing, and that is changing and moving, and yet I say why am I not moving. We have always assumed that we didn't want enough, right? That's why we constantly try to get in touch with needs and make ourselves need to kind of make up for not wanting enough. Now when you get unhappy, or feel you need something, that's just so you can reaffirm your determination to want it more. So, somehow you've recognized "I don't want it enough, because if I wanted it enough, I could have it." Where did that come from? That universal belief that if you wanted it enough, it could happen.

So we do have some facility there and we do flip back and forth between being special and being awful, between being good and being evil. And we kind of split ourselves and we say my body is the evil part, my mind is the good part and my mind is the bad part and my body is the good part, you know. And we flip flop back and forth. We try to keep our lives as dichotomous as possible. And to believe in good and evil and mind and spirit and body; essentially, to divide oneself. The me here and me there. The me here and now is quite distinct from the me I hope to be and I'm going to be and I am tending toward being, and I become aware of that difference. How do I account for it in my life? I am not what I want to be, I am, you know—I am not motivated, there's something wrong with me. I am base, I am materialistic, I am attached, I am needy, whatever. And I want to free myself from that because I am tending towards that.

You can't really be sure that you were doing what you want at the rate that you could be doing it, and that was your problem. Am I really doing my all? If I could rest assured that I was really doing my all, could I know any moments of unhappiness? If I really knew I was doing all that I could do toward what, though? Toward making people love me, toward being smarter, toward getting less messed up? We create all kinds of things that we can start believing we are doing all we can do toward. When I look ahead to see where I want to be and realize I am not there, I then look to explain why I am not there. To say that there is something wrong with me. Why isn't there any movement towards where I am going, why am I not there already? Why is there differential in my wanting and my being?

"Because there is something wrong with you."

If you knew there was nothing wrong with you, you wouldn't be wanting that which you couldn't have. For instance I wouldn't be wanting to be over there until I *was* over there. And then there would be congruity in my wanting. How would I get there? I wouldn't get there by asking what would be wrong if I never got there. However it is that I got there, it wouldn't be *because* I wanted to, it would be that I got there *and* I wanted to. They'd be the same thing. I would get there by wanting to be here first and wanting to be here, wanting to be here and wanting to be here, and that's how I would get there.

To summarize, why are you unhappy that you are not getting what you want? You believe you *should* be able to get what you want. And because you believe you *should* be able to get what you want, you must believe that you must have the power to get what you want. So there must be something wrong with you that you do not have what you want, and that's why you are unhappy.

If I was really flowing with it and congruent to all there was, I could be aware that I can make you be what I want you to be, only to the extent that I can. I can change you, insofar as I can change you, and that's fine, and I can't change you insofar as I can't.

If I believe there is something wrong with *you*, it always comes back as "there's something wrong with me." I have to suffer by my judgments.

What if you break that cycle, and end all so-called rational thought? You'd be some kind of an animal but it would be a new kind, it would be a human animal. Not "just" some kind of animal, but what you would be is that you would be the kind of thing that you were tending to be. You'd be the kind of thing that you were and perhaps we'd call that human, perhaps we'd call it angelic, perhaps we would call it base, I don't know. But that would all depend upon where we were. But you would be all you could possibly be, and knowing it.

You're wondering why you haven't got happiness and how to get it, because you want it, and that's how you know you haven't got it, sure. That is the most irrational thing in the world, you see. How could I want happiness if I had already had it? By not believing you had it. What you call better, you call better because you are already tending toward it. And that's your way of helping yourself get there, and you don't need any help. So, you are hoping that you could help yourself to get somewhere by calling it a better place to be, but that's only because you are going there in the first place.

I could say "I am going where I am going." And that would be a very full description, as total a description as I can imagine. And is it a better place? Well, I am going there. Is it an impossible place to go to? Well, I am going there.

The "have to's" are gone, the "should's" are gone, the choices are gone, but yet the choice is there. I'm really in touch that I am freely choosing to go there and also in touch that if I don't freely choose to go there, I am still going there.

When you are a therapist, you basically have people coming in and asking you, "What's wrong with me, and how can I be more of what I am, and how can I be more of what I want to be? And how can I move faster toward where I want to go? How am I keeping myself back from doing what I want? Why am I unhappy? I am unhappy you know and I am not getting what I want." And basically, what they are saying is there's something wrong with them.

I see the process as being a gradual one where more and more we allow ourselves not to believe that there's something wrong with me in this particular thing or in that area. Or as we work through the beliefs, and we decide we don't have to be unhappy, that we didn't really need to be unhappy, we don't have to be. That was a way of allowing ourselves to believe that in that case there's nothing wrong with me.

Where does the concept of karma come from? Where does the concept of falling from innocence come from? All of you are innocent. You just believed you weren't. Then the struggle back to innocence is to get back to where you already are, and you know it's somehow an impossibility, because you're there, but believing you are not and trying to get where you believe you are not. You keep trying to move on to some place that you are already at. If you are innocent but you believe you are not, isn't that as good as being guilty? Isn't that as good as karma? Is that the same as karma, really being there? If you are a happy person and you believe you are unhappy, isn't that as good as being unhappy? And isn't that the same as unhappiness exists?

The belief that there is something wrong with you is karma. The belief that there's something wrong at all. Freud thought that you could actually work in a chronological sense, let's say back to when you were two years old, and in each of those various stages when you plowed into another really big "there must be something wrong with me," that could be addressed. I don't see why it has to be chronological at all, because it's that you are doing it now. I think he was doing that because he believed there was something wrong with him too and them too. And this does not have to be chronological, but there is that sense of unraveling. We talk about it as peeling of an onion, but with many of my patients, I help them work on the one thing that they are unhappy about and lots of other unhappiness disappeared. So, we explain that by saying that the cause, the belief that was behind the one, when that was dealt with, it also dealt with all the other areas of their behavior that that same belief was behind.

I've asked my patients "What are you trying to get me to do for you? What are you trying to help me to get you to do?" And somehow, it always was "Give me permission so it'll help me find a way to give myself permission, to let myself be okay in these circumstances and to not believe that there is anything wrong with me, and yet know that I can still move, that to not believe something is wrong with me won't kill my movement. That allowing myself to believe that there's nothing wrong with me will not stop me from ever moving."

What are you afraid would happen if you didn't believe that there was something wrong with you? What you are afraid of is if you stopped believing that there was something wrong with you, that in itself might be because there was something wrong with you, that in itself may be a big mistake. And it would be proved that there was indeed something wrong with you. And so, if you stopped believing that there was something wrong with you, you'd *really* have to believe that there was something wrong with you. That it might be that what's wrong with you is to believe that there is nothing wrong with you.

Any schizophrenics, especially paranoids, that I've worked with, the ones that we consider the most disturbed, the ones that we say have the most wrong with them, are the ones that have attributed to just about everything in their life, that there was something wrong with them. You haven't done it with everything. Some of you have done it in more things than in others, but these people have done it in every little thing that didn't go their way. They said there was something wrong with them.

What do you grow up believing that is wrong with you? For a few years, you believe what's wrong with you is that you are small and then after a while you believe what's wrong with you is that you are a girl, there's always some reason to account for what's wrong with you. There must be something missing. And when you started getting all the things that you thought should cure you, what was wrong with you then? You are still not right. You've gotten money, you've gotten age, you've gotten whatever it was. Whatever "it" is really is not the cause of any unhappiness whatsoever.

Believing You Should Not
Have Been Who You Are

UNHAPPINESS is believing you should not have been able to be who you are.

For example, "I should not have been wanting or have been able to want this or that change in my life. It should have already happened so that I would not have to want it."

Unhappiness is believing you should have been able to be what you believe you were not able to be.

What does "should" mean? It means nothing, absolutely nothing. It is the word we have for adding nothing to our desires as a way of adding something to a desire that we have no desire to add anything to, other than its objective for extinction or fulfillment. It is supposed to aid in the fulfillment or elimination of the desire without adding anything to the attainment, the proper (natural) fulfillment of the desire's objective—that which is desired, the thing wanted.

Not Caring, and Freedom

In this talk, Bruce Di Marsico discusses caring and freedom.

Unhappiness is the belief that you're not free. In particular, that if you were happy now, you would be unhappy in the future. This is often a result of mistaking not wanting the consequences of an action for not being free to do the action. One particular form of freedom addressed is the freedom to care or not care.

Happiness is just you feeling your own desires, tastes, values, likes, dislikes, wants, and desires to avoid. Unhappiness is you feeling you and not liking you, and saying it's bad, that your desires, tastes, values, likes, and dislikes are not useful, practical, or beneficial to your desires, tastes, likes, dislikes, and values.

Our causing unhappiness is inadvertent, but it's inevitable when we cause it, and instantly remediable when we realized we caused it. There is no blame in being unhappy, any more than there is blame in flipping a switch you thought was a light switch, but is disconnected. It is a mistake, and as soon as you realize you were mistaken, you now know everything you need to know.

I'M not so concerned about why people have the dreams they have or why they wear the clothes they wear. It's why they're unhappy about it. But when you are starting looking at why people are unhappy about a thing, you really have to have the question of "Are you really unhappy?"

There are a lot of times you can help yourself or someone else by just asking, "Do you really care about that?" There are a lot of things people think they ought to care about, that they ought to feel bad about, that they ought to worry about, that they ought to be concerned about. And they've never felt allowed not to care about it.

But sometimes just the question, "Do you really care about that?" puts them in touch with, "Well, if I had to tell the truth, no, I don't." So now the unhappiness that they had is gone, partly because they thought they had to care and now they don't believe they have to care. But also the very act of caring was that when you really care about something, you have to be unhappy about it.

So now they don't have to care and they don't have to be unhappy about something, because they don't really care. They may still believe you only have to be unhappy about things you care about. You or I have to question, "How do you know if you're unhappy?"

We were talking about emotions are beliefs about future emotions. Now I know that that's not always easy to see because we're not used to seeing that way, but it is the basic underlying thing of why we got unhappy. The how is by making judgments.

Unhappiness is the belief that unhappiness can and will happen in the future. Unhappiness is the belief that you're not free. Unhappiness is the belief that you're not free, that you're not free to think what you think and you're not free to want what you want.

You're not free to not think something. You think you're not allowed to not think this or not want that, whatever you don't want, that you're not allowed to choose what you choose.

The whole concept of not being free means the punishment for being free is I'll wind up unhappy. Some people call it misusing your freedom. Some people call it abusing your free choice. Some people call it going overboard. There are all these names for why you'll be sorry later if you really feel free. "If you really believe you're free you'll be sorry" is basically what I'm saying. So unhappiness is the belief that you'll be sorry if you're free.

Fundamentally, feeling unhappy is the belief that you can be unhappy. Fundamentally feeling unhappy is the belief that you will be unhappy in some future, that you are capable of being an unhappy being. It is not feelings, but actually that you will have to see yourself in such a way as you call unhappy. You're an unhappy wretch.

Unhappiness is the belief that you do not have the right to be happy at certain times or under conditions determined by you. Now each thing I'm saying is another way of saying the fundamental truth about any unhappiness. I said unhappiness is the belief that unhappiness can happen, and will happen in the future. It sounds like I'm saying something different, though, when I say unhappiness is the belief you're not free, right? But the reason I can say it that way is that you're not free because you believe you'll be unhappy in the future, because you're afraid you'll be unhappy in the future if you are free to think what you're thinking, do what you want, choose what you choose. So it's basically the belief that you can be unhappy.

Unhappiness is the belief that you don't have the right to be happy. But if you ever ask yourself or anyone else "Fundamentally why are you not happy? Why are you unhappy when this happens or that happens?" they may say, "Well, it's not right." What they really mean is "I don't have the right. It's not right. I don't have the right to be happy. It wouldn't be right to be happy if this happened. I don't have the right to be happy. It wouldn't be right. I don't have the right." "It isn't right. I don't have the right. It isn't right. I don't have the right." Right means the ability to do something, and the fact of its consequences doesn't mean anything about the ability to do it. People often say you don't have the right to do that. What they mean is, "Oh, you can do it." Why would they tell you that you don't have the right if you really couldn't do it, right?

So it means you do have the ability, but you'll be punished. You'll be sorry. There are consequences that you won't want. But if there are consequences you don't want, that doesn't mean you don't have the right, right? It has nothing to do with rights. We may not want to do certain things because we don't want the consequences, but that doesn't mean we wouldn't say we don't have the right to do it.

So what could it possibly mean to say that you don't have the right to do something if you have the ability to do it? There's no meaning. But yet, people often say, "I don't have the right to do it," as if they don't have the ability to do it or the freedom to do it without feeling bad. I don't have the right to do it means then if I do it, I have to feel bad. I will somehow or another have to feel bad. Even if I don't feel guilty immediately, something else will happen that will make me sorry. So to believe that there is no right to do something is implying that there's going to be a punishment or consequence that you don't want, but that doesn't mean you don't have the right to do it.

If there's a consequence you don't want, then don't do it. The belief that you do not have the right when you have the ability is really your fear of the consequences. So anything you believe or feel that you don't have the right to do—the fact that you even make it seem that way to yourself and if you ever hear anybody else saying it—all you're really saying is you're afraid of the consequences.

You're not saying the consequences are undesirable, because if you made it that clear, you would say, "I don't want to do it because I don't want the consequences." You don't say, "I don't have the right to jump off the bridge." You say, "I don't want to."

If you really feel you don't have the right to be happy, you're really afraid of the consequences, but you're not saying that what you're avoiding is the consequences. Otherwise, if you were in touch with it, you would just simply say, "I don't want to do that because I don't want the consequences."

But if the fundamental problem of people is that they don't feel they have the right to be happy, and they're quite aware that what they really mean is they're afraid of the consequences, they might just as well say, "Well, I can't be happy. I shouldn't be happy. I don't have the right to be happy. I'm not supposed to be happy. It'd be crazy to be happy."

They could start putting in any kind of language, all the language that we hear. "Why the hell would I be happy when this happens or that happens? I'd be nuts if I was happy because that would happen. I don't have the right to be happy," which is really an expression of "I wouldn't want the consequences if I was happy," without any longer being aware that it's a choice. See, when you stop saying it's not a choice, "I'm choosing not to be happy because I don't want the consequence."

But the interesting thing about being happy is, if you thought that you could choose to be happy but would wind up with unhappy consequences, you couldn't choose to be happy. You'd be unhappy.

The funny thing, though, is that when it comes to unhappiness there are lots of things you wouldn't choose to do that you could do because you don't want the consequences. The consequence is just simply undesirable, but you don't say you don't have the right to do it. You just don't do it because you don't want the consequences. But when it comes to happiness, it's a little different because that's the be-all and end-all of your existence.

Happiness and you are fundamentally identical; they're one and the same thing. You are your happiness and you and your happiness are the same thing. When we talk about happiness, by the way, and say, "How do you know you're unhappy? How do you know you're happy?" happiness is just you feeling you. Unhappiness is you feeling you and not liking you, and saying it's bad.

When it comes to happiness and unhappiness, if you thought that you could freely choose to be happy any time you wanted, and thought, though, that the consequences for that is you'd wind up unhappy, we can't say that at that point you're really choosing to be unhappy in a sense, although it's true. But you couldn't really choose to be happy, could you? It's an impossible choice. You wouldn't choose happiness if it's going to cause you unhappiness.

You could choose other things that might have undesirable effects for one reason or another, for one benefit or advantage that you could imagine. But can you choose to be happy if you think the payoff is going to be unhappiness? Right then and there you're going to be unhappy right now, so how can you choose to be happy? Because you really think you have no choice. At that point you don't, you see. If you thought unhappiness was the inevitable and natural consequences of being happy, then there's no sense talking about choice because you couldn't have one. You'd just be unhappy about that whole situation. Every time you started to get happy you'd immediately get afraid of that because it's going to get you into trouble; it's going to make you unhappy if you're believing it's going to make you unhappy.

The first definition today: Unhappiness is the belief that unhappiness can and will happen in the future.

The second definition today: Unhappiness is the belief that you're not free because you'll wind up unhappy and then unhappiness will happen in the future. Being unhappy—now this is another definition—is simply believing about happiness that it will make you unhappy. It will make me—underline "make," naturally, inevitably, make or cause you to be—unhappy. So I'll say it a couple of different ways.

Being unhappy is simply believing about happiness that it will make me unhappy. Believing about thoughts, they will make me unhappy. Believing about loss, for instance, it will make me unhappy. Believing about desires, they will make me unhappy. Believing about actions, words, experiences, physical feelings, they will make me unhappy. Feeling about myself, others, nature, anything whatsoever can be believed to cause unhappiness.

So the fundamental truth here is that anything whatsoever can be believed to cause unhappiness, and you'll find that. So you can never be shocked, you'll never be surprised about what people can be unhappy about because anything whatsoever can be believed to cause unhappiness.

To summarize: People believe unhappiness happens and will happen. People believe unhappiness is caused against their will, but they cause it by believing this, by believing happiness is caused is how we cause it. You wouldn't choose to be unhappy unless you thought there was a benefit to it. So you would only choose to be unhappy if you thought by not choosing it you would be even more unhappy. So ultimately, you have to be believing you're going to be more unhappy.

So the idea of choice is lost in some sense, because of the belief that you're going to be unhappy. Everything follows after that. There really isn't much choice if you believe that you're going to be unhappy. If you believe that some thoughts of yours are going to make you unhappy or something that someone does is going to make you unhappy or could make you unhappy, if you believe that your not being unhappy could make you unhappy.

So if you believe anything could make you unhappy, you're going to be unhappy. So unhappiness happens if you believe that unhappiness can happen to you or will happen to you. That's how you get unhappy. People believe unhappiness is caused against their wills.

We're really talking about believing this happens against our will. Even though I'm showing you how we cause it, and how it's inadvertent, it's not against our will. It's inadvertent, but it's inevitable when we cause it. But it wouldn't be inevitable if we didn't cause it. But we wouldn't cause it if we didn't believe it was inevitable.

Unhappiness would not happen to us if we didn't believe it was going to happen. But we wouldn't believe it was going to happen if we knew that we caused it.

And we do cause it. It doesn't happen. But how we cause it is by believing it's going to happen to us. So it doesn't really happen to us. We do really cause it. But that's nothing to be afraid of because we only cause it by believing it's going to happen to us.

If you misunderstand what I'm saying, you'd say, "Oh, yes. We have learned from Bruce that we cause our unhappiness. Now I have to be afraid of causing my unhappiness when I don't want to, against my will."

You don't cause it against your will. You only cause it by believing it's going to happen anyway.

Exercise

This exercise is from the original group, as offered by Bruce Di Marsico.

Now this is the exercise. I want A's to ask three questions of B, regardless of their answers, okay? B I want you to answer as quickly as possible without hesitating with every question. Don't give it any thought. Just answer as quickly as possible because that's not important.

A, what I want you to ask B is: *What do people believe will make them unhappy?* And B will answer as quickly as possible. A, again, I want you to ask: *Why do people believe that, that thing that they just said will make them unhappy?* Answer that as quickly as possible. And then ask: *But why do they believe that?*

Okay. And then after you've done that, do it again, start again from right from the beginning: *What do people believe will make them unhappy?* And do that exercise two more times.

You Are the Authority on You

October 3, 1975

In this talk, Bruce Di Marsico discusses perfect self-trust.

All unhappy beliefs are derived from only one belief: Something can make you unhappy. You could only question yourself as to whether any symptom or sign in your body or your life could be unhappiness if you believed, in the first place, that something could cause unhappiness.

Believers in unhappiness define happiness as somehow unhappy (boring, unsafe, bad for their wants). Happiness is the absence of whatever doesn't belong there. If you do not want to be bored, then *your* happiness would certainly not be boring. If you do not want to be unsafe, then *your* happiness would certainly not be unsafe.

If happiness is seen as a way to ignore or avoid unhappiness, that is unhappy, because it is presuming there is unhappiness to avoid in the first place.

If you cannot trust your decisions, how can you trust your decision not to trust your decisions? You are the authority on you. There can be no greater authority.

ALL unhappy beliefs are derived from only one belief: Something can make you unhappy.

Even looking for the beliefs that cause the different manifestations of "unhappiness" is caused by not believing that *nothing* can make anyone unhappy. It is not believing that unhappiness was always "caused" or appeared to exist because people believed it was caused or happened to them (even if by their own behavior).

Because people were unhappy (believed that they could become unhappy) they were not really able to want to be happy. What they did do, though, was to fear unhappiness. Never did anyone believe that they wanted to be happy now or could be, or vice versa. Because of their unhappy belief about happiness (that it could be destroyed, annihilated, "lost" transient, etc.) it would have been contradictory (impossible) to even consider that unhappiness was purely a belief and nothing else.

People found it easier to believe in magic of the most fantastic sort; superstitions, gods, goddesses, raising the dead, flying saucers, devils, evil, monsters, turning lead into gold, reincarnation, final judgment, hell, heaven, etc. than to believe that they didn't have to be unhappy.

They could find it easier to believe in miraculous cures of ravaging diseases (at shrines, etc.) than to believe in the permanence of happiness.

Not that any of the above are either true or untrue; that is not the point. The point is that there has been no belief, no matter how foreign to personal experience, that man did not consider or even fervently propagate except that unhappiness is not caused by anything. The thought that nothing can make man unhappy, he only believed it could happen, has never occurred to an unhappy person. In fact, it could never occur to someone believing the opposite. Even if man wanted to know this, he would only experience his wanting as a fear of being unhappy.

Man's concern for doing or getting what he wants (his fear of not doing or getting), his not "feeling" like what he wants and vice versa, his not "knowing" what he wants, etc., are the results of the basic belief in unhappiness.

Wanting to know what, or why, or how, or anything about our present unhappiness or feared future unhappiness, is done when one is *not* believing that you do not have to be unhappy, *nothing* can make it happen to you.

The belief that some belief could make it happen can only be "true" when *not* believing that *nothing* can make it happen. Someone who believes that nothing can cause unhappiness knows that they could have no belief which could cause it. Only one belief can cause it for others—the belief that it could happen or is caused, or could exist, even in someone who believes nothing causes it.

To suspect or doubt or question yourself as to whether any behavior or symptom or thought or anything that comes in you or from you could be unhappiness is to be believing that something (known or unknown) is the cause of unhappiness. To wonder if some manifestation of your body (pain, pus, puke or perspiration) could be caused by unhappiness is the belief that unhappiness can happen to you.

This belief is not unhappiness, but is the cause of all behavior that it naturally produces, which believers in unhappiness call the experience of unhappiness.

Unhappy person means someone who believes that "happiness" can be lost and they could be unhappy. "Unhappy" *means* believer in unhappiness.

Unhappy believers do not believe that nothing can cause or make them unhappy, sad, afraid, feel bad, angry, etc. They do not believe that their own feelings cannot lead them into unhappiness. They do not believe that their desires could never lead them or cause them to be unhappy in the future.

Unhappy believers do not believe that happiness is really happiness. They believe it will make them unhappy if they accept it for the "wrong reason." They do not allow themselves happiness when it "shouldn't be" present according to their rules for avoiding unhappiness (which they develop in time according to the various circumstances). This is called psychological "reality" (by other unhappy believers). If their beliefs conflict with other protective beliefs of others they are considered psychologically disturbed. Degrees of disturbance are according to the degrees of disagreement with their rules.

Unhappy believers do not believe that unhappiness is really unhappiness. They believe that it will "strengthen" them against greater unhappiness. In a perverse way they agree that they can develop attitudes and experiences which do alter or modify their unhappy feelings in "unhappy" situations where they would be un-happier if they did not have the "right" attitudes.

Unhappy believers believe that unhappiness can lead to happiness and happiness can lead to unhappiness.

Unhappy believers do not believe their own definitions of happiness as "feeling and being the way one likes or wants" and unhappiness as "feeling in a way that one dislikes."

They say that happiness all the time would be "boring" (would that be happiness?) or would cause them to disregard what they want (happy state?). In short they say that many things are more desirable than happiness (which is precisely most desired) because they are more helpful in avoiding unhappiness (which of course, they would not have to avoid if happy all the time).

Since all that they believe, they believe in order to avoid unhappiness, it is impossible that they could be truly happy or even want to be.

They do not believe in perpetual happiness as even possible because they believe that unhappiness must be avoided while at the same time believing that it could never be completely avoided. This they must do. Believing that unhappiness could happen at all is an unhappiness that they do not want to avoid. They do not want to avoid that belief (even though they really do not want it) because they believe in it. They hold it as true. That belief alone accounts for the whole of what they call their experience of unhappiness.

Yet, although the thought or idea or revelation that unhappiness is simply a belief would never arise from their own "sets" or systems of belief, it does not mean it cannot confront them and occur to them from another cause. If in their environment the idea exists and meets their beliefs, something can and will happen. They will recognize a desire to accept the idea. If they believe it because they want to, then they will truly believe it. If they see it as true, a fact, a reality, and accept it as such, then, of course, they are now happy and by definition "know" that they never will be unhappy again (or actually they "know" they do not believe it exists for them anymore).

If they see it as a logical debate or something they need to be convinced of, it is because they do not believe it, because they believe unhappiness can still happen. If they see it as a way to avoid an unhappiness (or ignore an unhappiness) that they believe they "feel" or are experiencing, then they believe in unhappiness.

Anyone who says "but" in any way does not recognize it as true, of course. They simply still believe that unhappiness might happen anyway, no matter what they do (even no matter what they believe— although they didn't believe this truth).

All "unhappiness" comes from believing that people can become unhappy by being made unhappy or by being subjects or passive victims of a cause of unhappiness.

In one sense, no one can be unhappy (lose their happiness) and all that that means (evil, something wrong, etc.) but people have believed that it was an evident fact. People have believed it was a divine or absolute truth. That state of believing in something you don't want to believe in, no matter what form it takes, causes believing something to be true, and not realizing any longer that you don't want to believe it to be true. From then on, wanting and believing will be in conflict. Thence develops right and wrong, good and evil, happiness and unhappiness, etc.

Yet, people can call their feelings unhappy because they can think and act as if unhappiness was real. They can think that what they feel is caused by something they don't want to cause their feelings. They believe that something (mysterious or known) has the power to make them experience or reflect on themselves (or believe about themselves or feel in their bodies) in a way that they do not want to.

They believe that their bodies are controlled by forces that they do not want to have force over their bodies. They believe that there are things about themselves, or experiences of themselves, that are not natural to them.

Natural means real.

They believe that there are things that could be real about themselves that they believe would not be really be themselves. They believe that they could have real sensations (desires, movements, happiness) which they believe are not real. They believe that things are real about themselves that they believe (fear) are not real.

This whole disparity is expressed by a question like:

"Can I trust my decisions (judgments, desires, feelings, etc.)?"

The question is full of contradictions.

If they cannot trust, can they trust an answer to the question?

If they do not trust their decisions, who will they make the decision to trust?

Trust means "love," "be happy about" or some such thing. Or it means "accurately predict by means of" or some such thing.

Yet whatever it may mean, used in conjunction with one's own motivations, the term is meaningless.

The question means:

"Do I make my decisions?" or

"Do I believe my beliefs?" or

"Do I choose my choices?" or

"Can I do anything without me?"

Am I real?

Do I really want what I want? Am I against what I want?

Is the real *real*? Do I feel what I feel? Do I believe what I believe? Am I the authority on me?

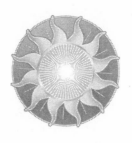

SECTION V

Fearing Unhappiness

Fearing Unhappiness, Is Unhappiness

B UT you're not going to get it by saying unhappiness is okay. See, because unfortunately unhappiness is something you don't like. You have to be honest and admit you don't like being unhappy. But that's all. Just admit you don't like it. There's nothing you have to do about it. You can't justify unhappiness and expect to be happy, but you can't fear it either. There's a problem with unhappiness. If you love it or you hate it you'll get unhappy immediately. By definition. A real problem. If you think it's good for you or bad for you, you're unhappy.

You're saying the way I don't want to be is good to be or is bad to be. No. The way you don't want to be is the way you don't want to be. When you've said you don't want unhappiness, that "I don't want it" reverberates through the ends of the universe. It reverberates to the high heavens. You have said all you could ever say when you say "I don't want it. No more of that." But when you say, "I hate it. I fear it," you cringe down to a pellet, to dust, to a dung beetle. You're nothing.

The truth is you can never stop being unhappy other than by wanting to be less unhappy. And somehow the idea has to occur to you, "I've had enough of this unhappiness. Maybe I can be less unhappy." And I'm sure that's what motivated anybody to seek help. But you can't call unhappiness bad in any way shape or form or you'll never be able to help yourself. In *any* way, shape or form. Not even slightly bad, slightly annoying, slightly disappointing. It just doesn't matter.

It's just a trick you're trying to play to make yourself not want to do it. And it doesn't work. You think that if you can just make yourself feel bad about it, you'll stop. And that's just wrong. Nobody ever learned by feeling bad. That's the secret that alcoholics don't share with anybody. That they try to cure their alcoholism by feeling bad about being an alcoholic. And all it does is make them want to drink. And if they feel guilty about having that drink, all it makes them want to do is have another one. And they don't tell people that. They don't tell people that feeling bad about drinking is what makes me drink. So they hope someone else will tell them but no one else will tell them that.

Being Self-Defeating

1970

In this talk, Bruce Di Marsico discusses beliefs that we can be self-defeating.

The only cause of unhappiness is believing that something can cause unhappiness. This "something" always ends up being ourselves. Unhappiness means that I believe that I do, or want, or think, or feel a way that is bad for me. All unhappiness is the fear that we have a bad attitude for ourselves, and the belief that we could in any way be bad for ourselves is unhappiness. In previous times, this belief was sometimes called "sin."

All fear is the fear of feeling bad (unhappy), which derives from fearing that we could act against our own interest. Since we could only know what is against our best interest by knowing what our best interest is, we are always in touch with our best interest, and could never act contrary to this knowledge. We can only mistakenly believe we have. Mistakes do not prove we are against ourselves, they only show that we have more to find out about the best way to be for ourselves.

Sadness is the acceptance of "proof" that we are against ourselves. It is the collapse of believing that "I am always self-defeating and will always be self-defeating."

Anger is believing that we are being made to be against ourselves. It is the explosion of believing that "you made me be self-defeating."

You are only unhappy because you believe you have to be. Your belief that you have to be is caused by your belief that something other than your belief could cause your unhappiness.

The cause of unhappiness is a belief; only one belief. What happens, no matter how undesirable or destructive to our life, health, desires or loves, does not cause unhappiness. The belief that we have to be unhappy is the only cause.

To state it simply:

If a person did not believe he or she had to be unhappy, they would not and could not be.

We merely believe we need to have things or avoid things in order to avoid unhappiness; which we would not have to fear if we did not believe we needed to be unhappy.

Belief Is Attitude Is Personality

A BELIEF, whether conscious or not, is an attitude. It is a postulate, presumed to be true, and therefore is an attitude held by a person which determines every aspect of the self that is pertinent to that attitude. Although a belief may not be, or ever have been, expressed in words or recognized as a personally held assumption, it is nonetheless held in at least a non-verbal way, and in all other psycho-physical ways as an aspect of the person; which we refer to as the personality.

What Unhappiness Means

When a person is believing he/she has to be unhappy, what they are believing is that they have to be unhappy because they believe they are against themselves. The belief in unhappiness is the belief in being wrong for oneself. Unhappiness, in fact, means that I believe that I do, or want, or think, or feel a way that is bad for me.

"Wrong" Thinking

A person believes: Certain things I do not want to happen may happen or are now happening. I don't want them to. I feel bad (and am worried or afraid now) because I "shouldn't" be thinking negatively about my life now. Maybe I shouldn't be not-wanting what is evidently happening anyway. It is as if I am denying reality, and that is wrong. I will be unhappy about this in the future because when certain things I do not want or do not like happen I will feel a way that is bad for me. It is wrong to expect misfortune. That is "unhappy" of me.

"Wrong" Wanting

It doesn't matter that if the undesirable event happens to me from circumstances out of my control, or if I think I am the cause or part of the cause; unhappiness comes as me believing that I now have proof that I am bad for myself. "Bad for myself" means I am not really wanting for me what I "should" be wanting for me, and something can prove it. The belief is that this event "proves" it.

"Wrong" Being

Basically, feeling bad means that I believe that what I do, or think, or want, or feel means I am against my own best interests. I believe these are a bad way of doing, thinking, wanting or feeling. The way I am being is a bad (wrong, self-defeating) way of being.

This could be called the same as believing that I will be a way I shouldn't be, or think a way I shouldn't, or want or feel a way I shouldn't. If we didn't believe that we could be a way we "shouldn't" we couldn't feel unhappy no matter what else we felt.

All unhappiness is the fear that we have a bad attitude for ourselves. We are afraid that something proves we are bad for ourselves in the sense that it is in some way against what we are for, and for what we are against. We are afraid that we have a self-defeating attitude.

"Wrong" Attitude

The fear that we have a bad, or self-defeating, attitude is the same as distrusting the very source or cause of our motivation. We are unhappy when we believe our very life, our heart, our self is against all that we live for; our personal happiness. Happiness is the freedom to be as we are, however we are; richer or poorer, in sickness or in health, gaining or losing, winning or failing, wanting or not wanting, approving or not approving, forever. Happy is what we are and what we'll be if we don't believe we are wrong to be as we are.

All Fear Is Fear of Unhappiness

Fear may be felt as anxiety or worry and other kinds of feelings which really are the anticipation of unhappiness, the anticipation of feeling bad.

All fear is the fear of feeling bad (unhappy). This is expecting being a way that we will then feel is wrong. It could be expecting to behave in a way we believe will prove we are against ourselves. We could fear being directly self-defeating (a "hysteric"). We could be expecting to be treated in a way we believe will prove we are against ourselves, or to have bad luck (a "paranoiac"). It could be expecting an undesirable event which is a combination of both the above. It could be the experience or the anticipation of a mysteriously caused, or random, accidental, bad luck which, we don't know how, but somehow it does prove we shouldn't have been the way we are.

Seems Like Proof

ALL unhappiness is caused by the belief in "proof" that we shouldn't be happy; which really means "proof" that we shouldn't have been free to have been as we were, which is why we are as we are. The undesirable incident "proves," "shows" or "makes it be" that we are bad for ourselves. The belief that we could in any way be bad for ourselves is unhappiness. Anyone who believes that is, by definition, unhappy.

We are either sad or angry at this proof. Sadness is the acceptance of such proof. Sadness is believing that what is proved is that we are unable to be other than against ourselves. We can't help it.

Sadness is feeling bad about losing something or someone we believe we need for our happiness. Without it we believe we have less "proof" of our goodness for ourselves.

Anger is believing that we are being made to be against ourselves, and it should not have been necessary for it to have happened at this time. We believe that not only are we against ourselves, but it was caused by our not admitting or expecting to be disappointed at this time. Anger is feeling wrong for not expecting to be wrong. We feel we fooled ourselves. People can seem to be angry at themselves or at another. We are really angry that we allowed ourselves to be mistaken. People are angry at being fooled when they "shouldn't" be. In short, anger is believing in being "tricked" into being self-defeating. The archetypical case is finding oneself being punished for doing what was believed was a "good" deed.

The Essential Characteristics of Emotional Events

Things to be happy about: Things that "prove" we are good for ourselves, or whatever takes away what "proves" we are bad for ourselves (even good luck).

Things to be unhappy about: Things that "prove" we are bad for ourselves, or whatever takes away what "proves" we are good for ourselves (even bad luck).

The things that can matter to happiness or unhappiness can be anything:

* thoughts or lack of thoughts,
* remembering or forgetting,
* desires or lack of certain desires,
* behavior or lack of behavior,
* events that happen to or are caused by self,
* events that happen to or are caused by another person or
* events that are caused by the absence of another person,
* events that happen to or are caused by the actions or attitudes of others.

In fact, anything that "means" whether we are good or bad for ourselves matters to happiness or unhappiness.

Happiness Won't Make You Do Anything You Don't Want to Do

WHEN you question your unhappiness, you're not looking to torture yourself some more to find out some more fault of your own. What you're looking to find out is what mistake you're making. In other words, what are you honestly believing that's wrong? That's all. Just what are you honestly believing that is inaccurate? Not what are you honestly believing that makes you an idiot, or what are you honestly believing that makes you at fault. You're not at fault. So one of the things we start with, with anybody we're trying to help with their unhappiness is that they're not at fault. I refuse to accept that any of my clients are at fault for their unhappiness.

But they are, indeed, the cause of it. But it's not wrong and it's not bad to find out that we're the cause of something that we were accidentally letting happen. If you found out you were mailing your rent check to the wrong person all the time, you might be glad to find out. If you found out that you were withdrawing money from your bank account when you thought you were depositing it, maybe you'd like to find out. There are lots of things that we might be making mistakes about that we were just ignorant about, and one of the things that we were always ignorant about was our emotions.

When our emotions didn't work the way the priests, doctors, and professionals told us they should be working, then we felt we were really in trouble, and that was scary. And that's when people seek professional help, when the suffering person is just tired of suffering and they want somebody who will finally help them. And that's all. So we never believe that the unhappy person is at fault. Because they're not. Even though they are inadvertently and unwittingly causing their unhappiness, they're not at fault.

We demystify unhappiness. Through The Option Method they look at ways they can be free of unhappiness. No, I don't have to be afraid of that. It won't make me do this and when I feel this way it's not going to make me throw myself off a cliff, when I feel that way it's not going to make me kill, when I feel this way it's not going to make me do anything I don't want to do.

One of the things that people can get to be very comfortable and reassured about is that they don't do anything that they don't want to do. You only do things that you want to do. That will take you really far just testing yourself, enjoying that, trying that out. Am I free to do this if I wanted to? Am I free to do that if I wanted to? Yeah, but I don't want to.

Unhappiness Is Not Wrong

November 21, 1992

Unhappiness Is Suffering

First, in the personal experience of it, unhappiness is suffering. Unhappiness is feeling bad. It is for many the feeling of experiencing evil in their lives. It is a distressful state for the person who is unhappy. Unhappiness is feeling, to some degree, helpless in the face of the "unhappy" event. People feel threatened, hopeless, confused, powerless, lost, or in some way that something is "really wrong." They can feel unlucky or otherwise vulnerable to whatever chance brings their way. They worry that they'll never know when misfortune will strike. They're scared, nervous to a degree, and probably "coping" every day, ignoring the fear in the back of their minds which we are all supposed to live with as a part of life. No one has all the power they need to make sure they will always overcome the things they fear. People suffer in their hearts and minds and bodies from the uncertainty of eventual unhappiness. The world of suffering people believes that some unhappiness is inescapable.

Unhappiness Is Not a Behavior

Although there are many kinds of unhappiness, each demonstrates the suffering of the unhappy person. If the behavior of the unhappy person is expressive of unhappiness, then it is. If the physical expression is not indeed an expression of an unhappiness believed in, no matter how it looks, then it is not unhappiness. Unhappiness is first and foremost, and only, a way of thinking. Although thinking for the human always has a physical counterpart, the physical manifestation (be it an interior feeling and/or an expressed behavior) is nonetheless caused by the believed way of thinking of the human.

Unhappiness Does Not Cause Unhappiness

In any case, no matter how unattractive an unhappy person may seem, or the expressions of unhappiness, no matter how dangerous they seem, unhappiness is still unhappiness, not evil.

Unhappiness no matter how expressed, or what kind, or style, or nature can never in itself cause further unhappiness, save to the fearful, and then it is their own belief that is the true cause. Although one kind, or many kinds, of unhappiness may touch on your fears or beliefs, it is still merely unhappiness.

People Do Not Cause Unhappiness

My point in stressing this is to warn against the error of believing that an unhappy person is a cause of unhappiness in others, or even to herself or himself. It is an error to think of unhappiness as a truth about a person. It is, of course, an error of belief of the person about herself/himself. The person as whole being cannot cause unhappiness any more than can any other thing.

Unhappiness Is a Belief Alone

It is the belief alone which makes the person experience what seems like unhappiness to herself/himself. If there is anything we know to be wrong it is the belief that is held by the person, not the suffering human. The belief in evil and unhappiness is not wrongfully held, the belief is what is wrong. It is held like humans are rightfully able to hold any belief they believe in.

It Is Not Wrong to Suffer

If we came across a broken, bleeding person who fell from a building, it would be a rare person who would believe that the person was wrong to be lying there suffering. We would not believe he was wrong to be suffering since he fell from such a height. We would not question his suffering. It is not wrong to fall down once you've slipped over the edge with no support. You may have believed that you will not have an accident, but will stand firm. It is a mistaken belief in this case, and there are consequences of being in error like this. The actual damage and hurt of falling is not the fault of the victim.

Holding a Belief

Once a belief (like the one about unhappiness) is held to be true it is held as a truth, not as if it were merely a belief. The truth that is indeed true is that unhappiness is merely a belief, and therefore it can be questioned authentically, innocently, and objectively. The objectivity with which we will question that belief is not to be considered contrary to the compassion and understanding we have of the suffering person. We do not in fact, and in reality, question a person.

We do not question their right to any thought or belief or way of being, or even their way of feeling. What we question is a belief. We, by questioning it, expose it as a mere belief that can, indeed, be questioned.

People Should Not Be Happy or Unhappy

To be impatient with unhappy persons because they continue in their unhappiness may be believing that people should rid themselves of unhappiness. That would be to deny or forget that they are unhappy because they believe it is a necessary and inescapable truth about themselves. That they don't have that belief is an impossibility. Who would or could ever be unhappy otherwise? All unhappy people believe it is necessary to be unhappy. That's why we ask, "Why . . . ?" etc.

Two Unhappy Beliefs

There are two judgments one can make about unhappiness. Either of them is merely another form of unhappiness. These two opinions of unhappiness are the perpetrators of unhappiness. They each make unhappiness seem other than what it is, and therefore perpetuate the mystery.

Unhappiness is simply what it is, no more, no less; no other than feeling a way you don't like. Unhappiness is not good, nor is it bad.

Not Good, Not Bad, Not Real

The belief that it is good only praises it, and proclaims a value and usefulness to that very most undesirable state that mankind has always wanted to escape. The belief that it is bad only promotes hate for it, and proclaims it to be something fearful and mysterious. Both attitudes fail to acknowledge that any unhappiness is merely a belief and an illusion of the unhappy, fearful person alone. It is not something real to fear. To fear that something is real does not make it real. It is, at most, undesirable: period. That we don't want it is the second most honest thing we can say about it. That it is not real is the most honest acknowledgment.

Praising the Captor

To praise unhappiness is to deny that we don't want it. It is like the Helsinki Syndrome. We have been captured by an enemy (which we believe is inescapable), so we try to come to good terms with our captor; even to loving it. The worst fear and greatest fantasy of escaped captives must be that their beloved captor may come to visit again and be welcomed with open arms.

Hate Is Fear

Likewise, to hate unhappiness is also to deny that we simply don't want it, and believe it is something, in itself, to fear.

To fear unhappiness is another fear. It will never eliminate unhappiness. To find good in unhappiness is also another fearful state wherein we condemn ourselves to believing we actually desire it, and therefore we will have to fear its reappearance whenever it might be "good" for us.

Choice

To believe that we either welcome unhappiness as a good, natural sign of our caring and sanity, or fear that we will be visited by unhappiness against our will are both the same unhappy belief. We have believed that it is good and naturally necessary to be unhappy; we believed we needed it to be saner, and therefore happier in the long run. We have, therefore, had to fear that we will get unhappy even when we don't want it, because it is natural to our desire not to be crazy.

Crazy vs. Happy

Because we have believed that happiness is antithetical to our values when we don't get what we desire, we have believed that if we maintain our desires in the face of threat or loss we would be crazy (somehow against ourselves) if we were still happy. That belief is what we question by using The Option Method.

The Truth

Therefore, the beginning point, the Great Truth we start with, is that we know that people believe that unhappiness is necessary, and that is why they are unhappy, but is almost beside the point to believe that people get unhappy, or make themselves unhappy. Maybe in some enlightened sense you might someday benefit in seeing it that way, but never instead of, or before, you fully understand that they believe they must be unhappy, and are suffering because they believe it is an inescapable truth. Unhappiness is simply believing; not being, or getting, or making, or doing unhappiness.

SECTION VI

Nothing Need Be Done
About Unhappiness

To Be Happy, Know This

To be happy, know that even though you cannot imagine your happiness in the future, you don't have to be unhappy today.

To be happy, know that:

1. You are only unhappy because of what you believe.
2. Your future happiness depends on no person or event.
3. If you stop believing in unhappiness, happiness will find you.
4. All sorrow is caused by unhappiness, not loss.

Sin

To believe in sin is to fundamentally believe that I am against my very self, my very good, my own future. Unhappiness is just a secularized belief in sinfulness, wrongness, and is the same as believing that we choose what we know to be wrong or bad for us. Like Adam and Eve we believe we know that which we are happy to choose can be really bad for happiness.

Mistakes Prove Nothing

Mistakes we make (if they are) are choices for what we want, and need not prove we can choose against what we want. We need knowledge or better information (if anything), not a change of heart. Our motivation is the best possible human motivation. Given human equipment, we want with human hearts and minds; with human brains and guts. We perceive and choose accordingly with human sensibilities, and only pay with what we have been given to pay with. There is nothing wrong with the way we work.

To get or keep what we want, even our lives, we need what it takes to do that. Sometimes it seems beyond our capabilities. That perception (whether true or not) is a function of our self-interest. Everything that is truly us is an aspect of our self-interest, and nothing is not. If things do not go the way we want it is not for the lack of our wanting, and therefore not from a lack of our best motivation.

You Can't Make Yourself Happy

THE truth of the matter is feeling bad causes feeling bad and it doesn't help us learn. Especially those things that are natural to us and that we want naturally. You can't try to sleep in order to go to sleep. Sleep doesn't work by trying. It isn't caused by trying. The whole concept of sleep is allowing yourself to sleep, permitting yourself that deserved rest. That's what makes sleep so beautiful. And if sleep's not beautiful; who wants it? So you can't make yourself sleep. These are certain things, there are certain phenomena in your body you can only do by allowing it to happen. And that goes for happiness. Happiness comes by freeing yourself up and just allowing it to be. If you're allowed to be happy, you'll be happy. The only reason you're not really, really, really happy now is because you're not really, really allowed to be happy now. That's all. Insofar as you're allowed to be, you will be and you are. That's all. It's that simple. And then you might want to look at why in the world would you not be allowed to be. It'll be funny but it'll still be real for you. And it'll be effective for you to look at, as long as you are willing to be happy.

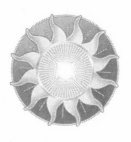

SECTION VII

Unhappiness Doesn't Exist

Summary: Unhappiness Doesn't Exist

U NHAPPINESS is not real. It would not even seem to exist except for one thing. The only cause of "unhappiness" is the belief that it is caused by something else other than your belief.

No One Is Actually Unhappy
December 1987

PEOPLE don't really ever get unhappy. They just only believe they're going to, and that belief is what they feel, which we then commonly call unhappiness. When you talked about total unhappiness, you have to understand, we're just talking about a belief. The behavior that we call the most extreme crazy behavior is often a person who believes that they're totally unhappy, thoroughly evil, and completely wrong. That's what you're going to see being acted out, but you're never going to really see any unhappiness, only the fear of it.

We commonly and practically refer to things and emotions as unhappy, and the feelings are real, but what they are believing doesn't have to be real. When someone is believing that something is very, very bad, they are unhappy, but "unhappy" is just shorthand for saying they believe something is bad. They're believing they're going to get unhappy, and that's what it feels like to believe you're going to get unhappy. Unhappiness doesn't really exist. People don't feel unhappy. What they feel is what it feels like to believe in unhappiness, what it's like to believe in "bad" or to believe in evil.

In summary, people have emotions about what they think they're going to feel in the future. Emotions *now* are about what you believe your future emotions will be. So, what they feel is what they think they're going to feel, but it didn't even happen. This is what it's like to believe you're *going* to feel it. Some people say they feel the devil in them. They can feel the demon. I want you to hear unhappiness as something like this: when people say they feel unhappy, it's like saying they feel the devil.

A person who thinks they're crazy is a little different. They believe they're feeling things they don't want to feel and doing things they don't want to do and having desires they don't want to have. They believe in craziness, and because they believe in craziness, they can find symptoms in themselves of craziness. But we only find symptoms of their believing in it. There's no such thing as a crazy person. A person with a religious background calls it feeling possessed. A person with a psychiatric background calls it feeling dissociated. The language is different but it's still saying that "I believe that I can be controlled by forces other than my own." It isn't possible.

The biggest mistake that anyone here could make is to believe that "Why are you unhappy?" means "Why the hell are you unhappy?" or somehow "You shouldn't be unhappy" or "There's no reason to be unhappy." To find out fundamentally, basically, what you're really unhappy about is sometimes to find out that you're not unhappy about anything. You can see yourself that what you're really afraid of, you don't even believe exists. You might propose, "I'm really unhappy. I'm really afraid that I will do such-and-such a thing," and you don't believe that at all about yourself.

I knew somebody who really did not want wealth, who said, "I do not want to be wealthy. I do not want to be rich." He said he hated the idea of being wealthy. I said, "Why?" "Because it makes you be an uncaring person, it makes you be a greedy person, it makes you be a whole bunch of unattractive things." I asked him, "Well, why do you believe that if you were wealthy, you would have to be those things if you didn't want to be?"

I didn't ask him that in order to make fun of what he believed. I just asked him why he believed it. Because there was nothing to the belief, when it came out in English as a real question, it just dissipated. He said, "I never asked myself that. I just always assumed." When you always assume something is true, you don't question. The whole value of questioning is to see if there's anything just being assumed, because where unhappiness is concerned, there must be an assumption that something is bad and that you're going to be unhappy.

There are lots of people in this world, everybody from the greatest scientists on down, who believe that there's always going to be some unhappiness in their life. Yet that belief is pure assumption and has nothing of truth in it. Your own unhappiness is a reason to question that. Why doesn't one question one's unhappiness even after the bitterness of it is known? Because another assumption is that it's good. Like any bitter medicine, you'll accept it as long as you believe it's good for you.

There are a couple of things that are conspiring and have been conspiring for millennia to keep people from questioning the whole assumption of unhappiness. Assuming there is unhappiness is an interesting play on words. Assumption means to take up; we talk about actors assuming roles, and if you assume unhappiness, you're taking it upon yourself. So there's a double meaning: Assuming unhappiness is like assuming a role. You've now assumed it, it's become part of you, it's you, and yet, assuming it also means it's never really you, but is only a role that you put on. It's an act that you perform by your own choice, and in that sense, it is *you* who is doing it, but the "unhappy you" is *not you.*

In other words, as an actor, I may be playing George Washington, but I am not George Washington. I am not portraying myself; I'm portraying somebody I believe is George Washington. So when you act unhappy, you portray someone else.

You Are Not Unhappy for Any Reason but Only Because You Believe You Can and/or Will Be Unhappy

March 17, 1975

No one was ever unhappy because they didn't get what they wanted. You were never unhappy because you didn't explore your beliefs. You were never unhappy because you believe what you do. You are unhappy because of one belief only: the belief that you are not naturally going to be happier. The belief that you aren't right now naturally motivated, moved by, living and doing everything you are doing from your happiness. The only reason you have ever been unhappy or anyone could be unhappy is that you believe that it is not happiness that rules you, that moves you, it is not happiness that directs your thoughts, your inclinations, your decisions.

The unhappy believe that if they didn't get "it," they will be un-happy—whether it be money, things, relationships, love, behavior from other people, behavior from themselves—they believe those are the causes of their unhappiness so they seek ways to control their own behaviors, to control the behaviors of others. They seek ways to control the world around them, all for the good of getting what they want. But it is why they do it that is why they are unhappy.

They do it because they believe they can't be happy unless they do it. Then if they didn't get that control, they feel bad and they say they should. They feel that they have failed and they believe that unless they succeed, they also can't be happy and they say their failure is the cause of their unhappiness. Since they don't do what they needed to do in order to be happy, they usually choose one of two ways: they blame the world and the way it is for their unhappiness or they blame themselves and the way they are for their unhappiness.

You have usually experienced both of them one time or another. Usually some of you find yourselves mostly on one side and others mostly on the other. Then you realized that a lot of the bad feelings you have had and a lot of the reasons you haven't been able to get and do what you have wanted was because you were afraid and so that you needed to get control over your fear in order to better get what you needed to be happy, in order to better be the kind of person that you needed to be, in order to be happy, and if you found that it was your fear that kept you from loving, then you worked on stopping being afraid, so that you could be more loving.

But we were always more concerned about being more loving then we were about not having the fear. If you found that it was your fear that drove people away from you—if you found that it was because of something you believed—you had a pain, and you always wanted to work on that belief so that you could get rid of the pain, so that you could draw the people closer to you, so that you could get those things that you needed in order to be happy. Always more concerned about what you were working towards than the fear itself.

Then you found out that the way to get rid of the fear was to change the beliefs, and there were times that the fear just made you feel bad, and so you didn't like the way that you felt, and you believed that if you continued to feel that way, you couldn't be happy. So you tried to get at the beliefs that would remove the fear that would get rid of the bad feeling. Still more concerned about getting rid of the bad feeling than you were about the fear. The fear was always one and the same: the fear that somehow naturally you would mislead yourself, that naturally you wouldn't be as happy as you could, that naturally you would believe things that would make you unhappy, that naturally you might want things that would make you unhappy, or naturally you would make the wrong decisions about what you wanted that would make you unhappy. Always believing that something about you naturally would make you unhappy, or might, but never quite fully believing that naturally, no matter what you say to yourself, no matter what happened in the world, no matter what you thought or didn't think—no matter what you did or didn't do—no matter what they thought or did—you never believed that naturally you would still be happy.

No one becomes unhappy because they do not do what they want or know what they want. We do not even become unhappy because we choose against what we want—if that were possible—or because we choose against what we seem to want—but we become unhappy from *why* we do not consent to our wanting—our possible wanting. We can only become unhappy because we believe we might become unhappy—that unhappiness is possible.

It doesn't matter what we believe is the cause or is going to be the cause of our unhappiness—it doesn't matter what we say the cause is. There is no difference if we believe we may become unhappy because of our wanting or because of our not getting what we want. There is no difference if we believe we could possibly become unhappy because we consent to our wanting or because we didn't consent to our wanting. If I believe that anything I do or want to do could cause me to be unhappy, then I am unhappy just because of that belief. Of course I would always want what I want and I would gladly consent to it unless I believe that my wanting could lead me to unhappiness. It is only *why* I go against my thoughts, feelings and desires, etc., that cause unhappiness. I am calling something bad. I am believing that my unhappiness can come from something in me or outside me.

We have always known that unhappiness came from calling something bad and what that simply means is that it comes from saying that there is anything that could cause me to be unhappy, that "bad" means could make me unhappy. So we don't use the word "bad," we may not use the word "bad" anymore, but if we still believe that anything could make us unhappy—that something could cause me to be unhappy—we are believing that something could cause us to be unhappy.

Why or what is it really that we are believing? We don't seem to be too discriminating. We just believe that something could cause us to be unhappy and we find one way or another of believing it. We will take something you constitutionally or physically believe and start with that—notice something about ourselves and we will say that is where it starts. I will be doing something and then say I should be doing something else. I will not be doing something and I will say I should be doing it. Feeling a certain way, thinking a certain thought and we start with anything that we can get our hands on, or our beliefs on. Is it because we have a natural propensity to do so? Is it because it is natural for us to just pick on ourselves? How about this: it is natural to discover that we are naturally going to be happy.

What does it matter if I could even knowingly go against what I want, which is impossible to do, until or unless I believe that I can cause my unhappiness; it just so happens that it is by definition impossible to go against what I want or not do what I naturally or happily would do, unless I am unhappy. I would always be doing what is coming from my life—from my happiness—unless I start believing that what is coming naturally from my being could lead me to unhappiness—non-being—the death of my happiness.

If you feel a pain—if you feel sick—if you feel a funny feeling—if you feel a sad feeling, an unhappy feeling, an angry feeling, any feeling—if your body—if you—feels in a way you don't want, what are you going to do about it? If you feel in a way that reminds you that you would prefer to feel differently, that is what I mean by "don't want." If you feel in a way that helps you to become aware that there is another way you would like to feel, that is natural, that is for you. What will you do with it? You have just become aware that there is another way you would like to feel. Will you naturally begin to feel that way—if it is natural for you? Well, will you naturally be happier?

If you know that you will naturally be happier, aren't you then and haven't you then done everything and the only thing that will make the difference—that will bring you to where you are naturally going? If your sickness, if your pain, is caused by your unhappiness, if your feelings are caused by your unhappiness—by what power or motivation would they ever get changed anyway? By more unhappiness or by the power of wanting to be happier, by the power that is in you—that urge that is in you which we call wanting to be happier, that life force, that thing called your desire?

Unhappiness Doesn't Exist

February 5, 1976

U NHAPPINESS doesn't exist in any way as an existent or being thing. It is a description of a phenomenon. It is an explanatory principle. The belief in its existence, and expectancy of it, is a dynamic phenomenon which inaugurates certain internal or external behavior (or intentional direction) which we can call unhappiness.

A belief or a judgment is a behavior from which, when initiated, will follow a course of behavior dependent on extra-personal phenomena. Once a belief is begun (a stance is taken), a direction is predetermined and will continue according to the determination (or intentional direction) unless changed. Various external phenomena will interact. The course will be modified and manifested according to the externals, but the direction will continue.

Real Unhappiness Could Never
Exist without Your Consent

June 12, 1975

You create (believe) "unhappiness" in order to prove that real un-happiness could never exist without your consent. You don't want to believe that unhappiness is impossible and can't be summoned no matter what you do. You want to believe that you have the power to make the difference. You want to know that if unhappiness does not exist, it is because of your decision and not because it would have to be that way anyway.

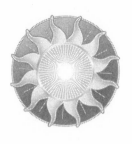

COMMENTARIES

by Aryeh Nielsen on

"Unhappiness"

Not Believing Yourself

This commentary represents the editor's synthesis of ideas Bruce Di Marsico expressed only in fragments.

THE cause of emotional stress is believing you don't want to do what you are doing.

If you knew you wanted to do what you are doing, how could you be stressed?

If you wanted to do something else *more*, you would do that.

If you change your mind about what you want to do most, or get in touch with some other want that you want to do more, you will do that.

Stress is not *consenting* to wanting to do what you are doing. It is not believing yourself that you actually want to do what you are doing.

Surrendering vs. Believing Yourself

The idea of "surrendering," often proposed in "New Age" thought, is that stress is caused by not wanting what is happening (often called, "what *is*"). The idea of surrender proposes that to not be stressed, the key is to want what is happening (instead of what you are wanting, which is something else).

If you do indeed change your mind so that you want what is happening, then you will not be stressed. But you love that you want what you want, and so, you would never want to change your mind about what you want (until you really do.) To believe that to be happy you must change your mind so that you want what you don't want, is to pile unhappiness on unhappiness.

Trying to not want what you want ("surrendering") is in some sense an opposite of fully acknowledging (consenting) to yourself that you want what you want, of believing yourself that you really do love what you love.

Taking Responsibility vs. Believing Yourself

The idea of "recognizing that you are choosing what you do," or "Taking Responsibility," a concept often proposed in various streams of American self-help movements, is also a form of not believing yourself. Many of these movements also often propose that happiness is a way to being wealthy, so you can really be happy.

In so far as you are choosing what you are choosing, it is because of what you believe. As long as you believe what you believe, you will choose what you choose. But choosing, in this sense, is not an act of will, it is merely doing what you want most, given what you believe. "The Will," in fact, is the mythical assertion that there is what you want, and then there is what you really want, and some sort of effort must occur so that you can act on the basis of the latter instead of the former. But you could never do anything except what you are in touch with wanting most. There is only what you really want, which is the equivalent of saying that there is no such thing as what you really want, hidden in some depths.

The philosophy of "taking responsibility" is equivalent to the alternate self-reprimand, "Why the hell am I not choosing to do what I know I should?" and the self-praise, "Thank God I am choosing as I should." The idea that you choose your actions in this sense can only occur if you believe you could do something besides what you want to. If you know you are always wanting to do what you are doing, what choice is occurring?

Trying to choose what you want ("taking responsibility") is in some sense an opposite of fully acknowledging (consenting) to yourself that you want what you want, of believing yourself that you really do love what you love, and that there is no choice to be made.

The Experience of Unhappiness

This commentary is a synopsis of ideas that Bruce Di Marsico expressed in many writings or talks, but did not express summarily in a single writing or talk.

UNHAPPINESS always has an emotional feeling. Those beliefs we hold that are, for us, practical beliefs, have no emotional feeling. If there is a belief, and it has no emotional feeling, then we cannot experience it as an emotional problem.

> Unhappiness is what it feels like to *try* to believe a way that you don't.
>
> BRUCE DI MARSICO

A belief is a whole-body attitude. Unhappiness is the experience of having one attitude and *trying* to have another. When you are actually changing attitudes, there is no feeling of unhappiness. Consider experiences with a food that you used not to like, but like now. You didn't try to like the food. At some point, you discovered that you liked it. You can never force the issue by somehow making yourself like the taste of food that you don't like the taste of.

The feeling of unhappiness is the feeling of trying to have a taste for values that you don't have a taste for. You may be converted to new values, but *trying* to be converted has nothing to do with actual conversion. At root, the feeling of unhappiness is the most subtle feeling of being against yourself: of trying to have values that you do not have, which is the most root (and minute) feeling of dilemma. "I am bad" is "My values will somehow lead me to act against what I value," an impossible action.

> Happiness is not believing that what you feel is perfectly reflective of all you know.
>
> BRUCE DI MARSICO

As a corollary, unhappiness is believing that what you feel could somehow not be perfectly reflective of all you know (and hence needs to be changed.) You would never *not* act on the basis of all you know.

When you actually want to change values, this is always perfectly simultaneous and coincident with actually changing values. Bodily patterns of behavior may take time to be fully conformed to your values, but if your behavior apparently doesn't match your values, this doesn't mean you don't value what you do value.

Unhappiness Doesn't Exist
but *Is* Experienced

This commentary is a synopsis of ideas that Bruce Di Marsico expressed in many writings or talks, but did not express summarily in a single writing or talk.

THERE was a time when many thought they suffered from demon possession. They did not. Demon possession does not exist. They suffered from the belief that demon possession existed, and was happening to them right now.

No one suffers from unhappiness. What is suffered is the *experience* of believing that unhappiness exists, and is happening right now. *Unhappiness* doesn't exist any more than demon possession does.

The *experience* of being demon-possessed exists (for those who believe that demon possession exists), but *demon possession* in itself doesn't exist. Similarly, what people who *believe* that unhappiness exists call "unhappiness," is their *experience of believing* that unhappiness exists.

Happiness is valuing what you value.

It is (logically and inherently) impossible to not value what you (do indeed) value. You can, though, believe that you do not value what you value. What is called "unhappiness" is the (non-existent and impossible) phenomenon of not valuing what you value, or being "possessed" by values that are not yours.

Since all can only value what they value, and never can *not* value what they value, no one can ever be "possessed" by values that are not theirs—but they can *believe* they are, and they will experience this belief as unhappiness.

When people say they are unhappy, they are referring to their experience of *believing* in unhappiness, i.e., their experience of believing that they could value, or are valuing, what they do not value. They truly feel "unhappiness-possessed," but it is no more actually happening to them than being "demon-possessed" actually happened to anyone many centuries ago.

Acknowledgments

MY DEEPEST THANKS AND GRATITUDE TO THE MANY HANDS THAT helped birth this book. Aryeh Nielsen had the vision for this project; without his ideas, archival preservation work and enthusiasm, this book would still exist only in our imaginations. Richard Banton caught all of the big mistakes as we began to work with the raw material. Wendy Dolber, Bruce's student and friend, spent months reviewing; her watchful eye, editing skills and comprehensive understanding of Option was essential in making sure we "got it right." Frank Mosca's further review, editing and feedback was invaluable and put me at ease, knowing we had not missed anything important. I'd also like to thank Frank for his Foreword for this book as he so eloquently captured how so many of us feel about Bruce's work. Finally I would like to thank all of The Option Method students the world over who have patiently supported our efforts.

Deborah Mendel

The Editing Process

BRUCE DI MARSICO PRIMARILY TAUGHT IN A GROUP CONTEXT. HE often wrote short essays as seeds for group discussion, and would read the essay at the start of gatherings, followed by interactive discussion and commentary.

These essays sometimes were descriptive, and sometimes were poetic meditations. Bruce also wrote some essays for personal use, working out how best to convey an idea or to communicate to a particular person about a particular issue.

Bruce primarily worked through the spoken word, not the written. He recorded tapes of group gatherings from the 1970s through the 1990s, and over 500 hours of tapes exist. This represents an overwhelming amount of material, and so this work contains only a selection of materials from these tapes.

Both written and verbal works have sometimes been edited quite a bit for presentation here. While some pieces are exactly as written, others may have been modified by removing secondary themes to create a more focused essay, by weaving together two essays or talks on the same subject, by cutting whole sections of interactive discussions, or by adding a few extra words to clarify what did not need to be clarified in the context of an ongoing discussion. The principle was to only do what could be done with the confidence of maintaining the integrity of his authorial intent, as judged by some of Bruce's closest students.

The commentary sections in these volumes are to bring forth points that are felt to represent Bruce's ideas but for which good source material could not be found for using Bruce's own words. Some commentary is a synopsis of ideas that Bruce Di Marsico expressed in many writings or talks but did not express summarily in a single writing or talk. For example, a wide-ranging discussion about a topic over six hours of tapes might leave a very clear impression of Bruce's teachings on a subject, but present a great difficulty in extracting his word directly into a short, relatively linear essay.

Other commentary represents the editor's synthesis of ideas Bruce Di Marsico expressed only in fragments, such as intriguing short asides. In this case, there is more editorial extrapolation.

Finally, some commentaries are based on the editor's understanding of Bruce Di Marsico's teachings, often created in response to common misunderstandings of Option. These commentaries are not directly traceable to Bruce's words but may be edifying nonetheless.

The relationship of a given commentary to Bruce's work is stated at the opening of the commentary. Additionally, whenever an essay or talk can be traced to a particular date (and the vast majority can be so traced), the date is included so that future researchers of the archives of Bruce's material can easily check the edited version against the original.

The archives contain great quantities of materials that are wonderful and valuable, but were not presented here both for the sake of limiting the size of the volumes and not delaying their release by a period of decades! What is *not* here is the complete history of Bruce's playing out of Option in all the lived situations that actual people brought to him.

On that point, since Bruce often used a questioner's own language, a given talk might use a given term very differently than another talk, because the talk was in response to a different person. The context will make this clear.

As we continue to research the archives, and respond to questions for clarification, subsequent editions will invariably be created. Yet what is collected here is unquestionably more than sufficient for a complete understanding of Option. Enjoy!

About Bruce Di Marsico

BRUCE MICHAEL DI MARSICO WAS BORN IN 1942 IN WEEHAWKEN, New Jersey. He was the first child born to Onofrio (Alfred) Di Marsico and Elizabeth (Bette) Bauer. In their first child they found an exceptionally bright and precocious boy. While Alfred tried disciplinarian methods, Bette turned to Dr. Spock in raising him. As he grew older he became so adept at reasoning with his mother when he wanted something that it became obvious it was she who was learning from him.

Bruce was a restless child in school and was advanced a grade in elementary school after being tested by a psychologist. When it came time to attend high school he requested that he attend a Catholic school. He was drawn to a spiritual quest at a very young age. Upon graduating high school he was still seeking an immersion in theological study and chose to pursue a monastic life. He entered the Trappist order. After spending some time there as a novice he realized it was not the right path for him.

He decided to attend university and explore psychology and philosophy. He was fascinated by mankind's eternal pursuit of happiness. He thoroughly enjoyed the spiritual passions of the heart and soul. He always kept a volume or two of Butler's *The Lives of the Saints* at his bedside, loving the mysteries of the mystics. It was through his own quest for happiness—the same desire that drew him to Catholic school, the monastery and the study of the works and teachings of many from Buddha to Freud—that he came to create the Option teachings and Attitude. However, it was because of the joy he derived from helping others that he naturally came to develop The Option Method.

Bruce drew upon the wisdom of ancient philosophers. It was the Greek philosopher Epictetus who said, "Men are not worried by things, but by their ideas about things. When we meet with difficulties, become anxious or troubled, let us not blame others, but rather ourselves, that is, our ideas about things." Bruce realized it was not what was happening that made people unhappy, but their beliefs about what was happening that created their emotional responses. He developed his Option Method Questions based on the Socratic Method of teaching using non-judgmental questions. The theory of recollection, according to Socrates, means that before we are born we possess all knowledge. We are never taught anything new, but instead are reminded of things we already know. Bruce felt this was true about our happiness. He believed that every one of us already possesses everything we need to be happy.

Bruce became a psychotherapist, and around 1970 introduced Option at a paraprofessional school called Group Relations Ongoing Workshops (GROW) in New York City. Bruce's classes became "standing room only" as he taught laymen and practitioners from a variety of backgrounds his Option Method. Over the years Bruce offered various workshops and groups in and around New York City, Long Island and New Jersey. When GROW closed, a group of students asked him to continue teaching them. He created what came to be known as the "Monday night group" at his home in Montclair, New Jersey. A closeness and camaraderie developed among them and oftentimes discussions would carry on into dawn with breaks for fettuccini alfredo, family style, in the large eat-in kitchen. You will find transcripts of recordings of these groups throughout this book.

In the 1980s and 1990s Bruce continued to conduct workshops and groups from his home in Montclair as well as seeing private clients in his office in Greenwich Village, New York City. You will also find material from these workshops within these pages. It was during this time that Bruce was diagnosed with heart disease and later diabetes. Through years of physical pain and suffering, he continued to teach as he did in his last recorded lecture on November 11, 1995, transcribed in these volumes. Bruce was a testament to his own Option realization that pain itself cannot cause us to be unhappy. Bruce passed away on December 4th, 1995, with several of his last students at his side.

Deborah Mendel

Index

Breinigsville, PA USA
07 February 2011
254932BV00001B/4/P